T0300974

HOW TO BE A HAPPY TEACHER

Are you a stressed teacher? Do you feel overstretched by the responsibilities of the role? Are you suffering from poor work-life balance?

How to Be a Happy Teacher acts as a lifeline for teachers navigating burn-out, guiding them towards a happier and more sustainable experience of teaching. Written in an accessible style by Rachel Boucher, an experienced primary school teacher, her guide offers insights and actionable self-care strategies to improve teacher happiness within our schools.

The book is divided into two distinct sections: Part 1 unpacks crucial aspects of the teaching role, including, but not limited to, acceptance, purpose, prioritisation, self-care, and Ofsted. Part 2 shifts the focus to real life examples and exercises, providing teachers with the tools to address the challenges identified within Part 1.

Whether you're a seasoned educator or just beginning your career, this empowering guide provides the insights, camaraderie, and inspiration you need to succeed within this challenging yet rewarding career.

Rachel Boucher is a primary school teacher with over ten years of experience working within the field. She has acted as a lead in mental health and well-being, PSHE, music and English as an additional language within various primary schools, and has delivered training to colleagues on these topics.

HOW TO BE A HAPPY TEACHER

A Practical Guide to Self-Care and Wellbeing in the Classroom and Beyond

Rachel Boucher

LONDON AND NEW YORK

Designed cover image: © Getty Images

First published 2025
by Routledge
4 Park Square, Milton Park, Abingdon, Oxon OX14 4RN

and by Routledge
605 Third Avenue, New York, NY 10158

Routledge is an imprint of the Taylor & Francis Group, an informa business

© 2025 Rachel Boucher

The right of Rachel Boucher to be identified as author of this work has been asserted in accordance with sections 77 and 78 of the Copyright, Designs and Patents Act 1988.

British Library Cataloguing-in-Publication Data
A catalogue record for this book is available from the British Library

ISBN: 978-1-032-82906-7 (hbk)
ISBN: 978-1-032-82901-2 (pbk)
ISBN: 978-1-003-50691-1 (ebk)

DOI: 10.4324/9781003506911

Typeset in Interstate
by Apex CoVantage, LLC

For Mrs Piddington, who cared.
For Mrs Baxter, the greatest headteacher there ever was.
For Dr Andrew Fisher, who 'got me'.
For Amanda Cockayne, who listened.
For all of my incredible colleagues over the last decade.
For all the teachers, everywhere.
Especially for those who think they never made a difference.
Trust me, you did.

CONTENTS

viii   *Contents*

PREFACE

I began writing this book while at the height of my teaching career. I was in a new school, with high hopes and even higher expectations of myself. I had been teaching for eight years, and I was confident in a job I knew I excelled in. I had a sense of purpose, and I knew that I was making a valuable and positive difference in at least 30 children's lives a year. By the end of the book, I was working a strange hybrid of two days in a permanent position, with supplementary days supply teaching, to allow me the flexibility to write. This gave me a valuable new perspective on teaching, as I was able to travel around, experiencing different settings, while still maintaining a job in a 'home base school'. It also allowed me to speak with several teachers about their well-being and the things they do to manage it in such a challenging profession.

'What's so difficult about teaching, then?' you cry. Ah, perhaps you're the spouse or family member of a teacher who has given you this book in a last-ditch attempt to make you understand that you don't 'just colour in' all day if you're a reception teacher, or that you don't 'finish work at 3 pm'. So for the uninitiated, here is a breakdown of the current challenges for teachers in 2024 Britain.

Exploring the complex landscape of teacher happiness

The quest for teacher happiness demands an understanding of the multifaceted challenges that create the labyrinthine structure of education. The dichotomy of relentless demands and the intrinsic joy derived from moulding young minds creates a dynamic tension that defines the teaching experience.

1. The unyielding demands of education

Teaching, at its core, is an undeniably demanding profession. The demands extend beyond the traditional boundaries of school hours, infiltrating weekends and holidays. Unpaid overtime becomes an unspoken norm, a silent sacrifice made in the pursuit of providing quality education. The profession, designed to be noble, occasionally veers into the territory of exploitation, where the goodwill of educators is stretched to its limits.

The pandemic, with its unprecedented challenges, thrust teachers into an even more precarious position. Accusations of laziness and abandonment pierced through the collective psyche, creating an additional layer of stress for educators already grappling with the complexities of remote teaching, health concerns, and an ever-evolving educational landscape.

2. *Financial realities and professional qualifications*

The financial aspect of teaching often emerges as a sobering reality. The misalignment between the hours invested and the financial remuneration received raises valid concerns. Many teachers, armed with qualifications tailored for the educational arena, find themselves tethered to a profession that, despite its intrinsic rewards, fails to offer financial incentives commensurate with the commitment required.

The question of professional qualifications becomes a pivotal factor. Degrees and experiences that once seemed like stepping stones to a fulfilling career can, over time, feel like shackles limiting options. The challenge, then, becomes finding avenues within education where these qualifications can be leveraged to create a more balanced and sustainable teaching experience.

3. *The paradox of criticism and passion*

Teachers navigate a delicate balance between passion for their craft and the paradoxical nature of criticism. The profession, built on the foundation of nurturing future generations, often finds itself subjected to external scrutiny and unwarranted accusations. The absence of regular praise and the omnipresence of criticism can cast a shadow on the intrinsic joy derived from witnessing a student's academic or personal growth.

The pandemic-induced accusations of 'lazy teachers' underscore the broader societal misunderstandings about the challenges faced by educators. It becomes imperative for teachers to reconcile their passion for teaching with the external narrative, finding solace in the impact they make despite the lack of public acknowledgement.

4. *The essence of teacher happiness*

Amid these challenges, the essence of teacher happiness emerges as a nuanced tapestry woven from various threads. It's a delicate balance between acknowledging the struggles and finding moments of joy within the profession.

Teaching, at its core, is a deeply human endeavour. The connections forged with students, the aha moments of understanding, and the transformative power of education create pockets of joy within the broader landscape.

So why did I feel qualified to write a book about self-help for teachers? Was I a perfectly happy, contented teacher eight years into my career? No, however, I did feel at this point as though I had a large amount of it 'figured out'. I had made all the usual mistakes early on, mentored tens of students, learned a great deal from my colleagues, and seen enough Ofsted inspections to understand what all the panic was about (and how to panic less about it). Amongst all this, I discovered the most important element of teaching, besides, obviously, the children. The key part of teaching, I have found when preserving one's sanity, is the camaraderie between you and your colleagues. They are the only ones who will truly understand the complexities and demands of what you're going through and why you continue to work harder than you should, despite not being paid to do so. Therefore, this book is not just full of my own tips and my sole ideas but also things I have picked up from hundreds of other wonderful, experienced teachers. I begin to delve into scientific research, as we teachers love to do, and also intersperse many personal excerpts from my career and my friends' careers in teaching, with permissions, of course, and names changed. The purpose of this book will be different for different people. For example, for your SLT (Senior Leadership Team, aka 'Management') members, it may be that they purchase this to check a box under their well-being bracket. Cynical? Perhaps. But am I wrong? Now, this is where the real purpose of my book comes in. Don't get me wrong, I hope that academies buy this up in abundance so that I can become the next successful author of self-help books, even if it is just to tick their well-being box. However, that is not why I wrote it. I wrote it for myself. I wrote it for you. I wrote it for my friends. I wrote it for that teacher down the corridor who never speaks to me or anyone because she hates her job and wants to die. I especially wrote it for her.

This is not another book that SLT makes you read and think your life is fixed. This is a realistic guide. It acknowledges, first and foremost, the impossibly incredibly difficult job that is teaching. It doesn't pretend that it's all sunshine and rainbows, with everyday beautiful and different and varied and vomit-free. So there's that. Secondly, the guidance it gives you isn't the sort of guidance I have read in these sorts of books before. For example, 'just do some more exercise', 'eat healthy lunches', 'organise a bowling night'. These are lovely but largely pointless ideas. Don't get me wrong, we appreciate a good night out, but this is a plaster on a problem that needs healing, not just covering up. The advice in this book, unlike in other idealistic tomes, does not require you to have ten extra adults in your classroom to realistically achieve. Moreover, it focuses on ways to address how you react to a situation that you cannot really change. 'The situation' being teaching in this country. Because realistically, there is nothing I can write that will make your job any less impossible. There is nothing I could say that would suddenly make it easy or bearable, even for some of you. However, what I do hope to do is alleviate some of your guilt, burden, stress, and thoughts that you just can't do it anymore. Don't get me wrong; if by the end of this book you still want to leave teaching, that is absolutely your right, your decision, and you shouldn't feel any shame in that whatsoever. But I do hope that by the end of this book, you are at least proud of yourself for every second you have spent in this impossibly difficult, life-changing profession. Because without you, the lives of children would not have been better changed.

Part I
Teacher life lessons

Making the bold claim of unlocking the secret to teacher happiness might sound like a whimsical notion, especially in an educational landscape where workloads have spiralled, and the once-sturdy foundations of teacher retention are now as fragile as autumn leaves. With a decade's worth of experience in primary schools, I find myself at the crossroads of relentless challenges and a profession that seems insatiable in its demands. The question lingers: How can one find happiness in a job that seemingly thrives on stretching our time to its limit and sapping our precious human energy?

Teaching, in its current form, is a demanding taskmaster, a relentless force that extends its tendrils into the realms of unpaid overtime and weekend administrative tasks. It exploits the inherent goodness of individuals who choose to dedicate their lives to nurturing the minds of other people's children, extracting more than they have to offer. The echoes of Sunday afternoons filled with worry, planning, and preparation for the week ahead resonate across staff rooms, creating a chorus of educators grappling with the weight of their responsibilities.

The statistics around teacher retention are telling, with a significant exodus in recent years, leaving the profession wounded and depleted. Conversations among seasoned teachers often carry cautionary tales, discouraging potential trainees from entering a field that appears more like a marathon of endurance than a fulfilling career. Yet despite the challenges, many teachers persevere. But why? The cynical answer might be that they lack qualifications for alternative careers that can sustain mortgage payments. It's a bitter truth for those armed with degrees and a wealth of experience, their qualifications seemingly confined to the narrow alleyways of education.

Critics may point to the financial discrepancy between what teachers are paid and the hours they invest - a stark reality that could make any prospective educator think twice. It's a profession where praise is a rare visitor, and criticism, whether from parents, superiors, or the public, seems to be an ever-present companion. The echoes of pandemic-related accusations, labelling teachers as 'lazy' and 'abandoning our youth', reverberate through the collective memory. These accusations, unfounded and unfair, were hurled at a profession that, against impossible odds, transitioned to remote work while continuing to support key worker children and vulnerable youth, even at the risk of personal health. It seems to have been forgotten that teachers even died during this period, from COVID-related ailments, because they too were on the front lines.

DOI: 10.4324/9781003506911-1

Amidst this challenging panorama, I boldly proclaim, 'Be happy!' Teaching, despite its trials and tribulations, stands as the greatest job in the world. Allow me to unravel the intricacies of this seemingly paradoxical statement, inviting you to join me for a reflective journey into the heart of education.

Part I - Teacher life lessons

Rationale: To improve staff well-being through concise lessons designed to be delivered weekly. Reflection sheets will not be provided, rather staff are encouraged to think about these lessons without adding additional workload or evidence.

Lesson 1   Acceptance

Lesson objective: To learn to accept the position we are in, concerning our chosen career path.

Steps to success:

- Embrace the fact that no one else gets it
- Know that you are enough
- Find the moments that remind you why you're here

It is a misleading and upsetting trope that teaching is a 'fall-back' career. Teaching is a carefully selected way of life. You can't just 'fall into' something that takes up the vast majority of your attention. It is a lifestyle choice, a commitment, a relationship that will always be more take than give, and it will define who you are as a person for years to come. So why does this trope persist? Teaching is a hugely misunderstood career. Despite teaching for ten years, I'm still fairly certain that my dad thinks I start work at nine and go home at three. The children in my class certainly do. Their parents seem to, as well, except for those who also teach. Teaching, however, demands (usually) an 8:00 am start at the latest, with the end of the day ranging from 4:30-7:00 pm, depending on your role, demands, and organisational skills. After years of trying to explain this to people, I have decided that the easiest way to be happy about this is to simply understand that other people will *never* understand this. It's frustrating, it's unfair, and it's polarising, but you can never show someone the unique challenges of teaching without forcing them into the career yourself. It's like trying to convince your reception class that you don't live in the cupboard. They will never truly understand - even if they see you in the supermarket, mouths open and eyes wide - their brains simply cannot compute that you have a life outside of school. So just let it be and know that the truth is your own special treasure. It's easier said than done, but there are several ways you can go about this.

Mrs Boucher's guide to 'letting it go'

Step 1:   If someone has said one of the following, don't immediately slap them:

- o 'You teachers get too many holidays!' - a parent of a child in my class
- o 'Don't you only work until three?' - a family member
- o 'You teach reception? Oh so you just dress up and play all day.' - a Year 6 teacher
- o 'I wish I got paid as much as you for babysitting.' - a former friend

DOI: 10.4324/9781003506911-2

Step 2: Take a breath.

Step 3: Calmly, and logically, correct their mistakes.

Step 4: If step 3 is unsuccessful, realise that you aren't going to be able to change their mind and mentally remind yourself that you're doing a great job and don't require their approval.

Step 5: Repeat. Probably weekly. Cast your mind back to those parents who, during the pandemic, while home-schooling their children, told you that they finally *got it* and appreciated everything you did (only to instantly forget once everything went 'back to normal').

While this may take practice, particularly with people you have to see regularly, it isn't worth your negative energy trying to convince the inconvincible. You can just know, deep inside, that the only people who will truly understand your struggle are those who share it with you. That's why it's so important to have work friends. Your work friends will *always* understand, and it's vital to be there for one another. It's also important, however, not to fall into a negative cycle when complaining about work – but more on that later.

Unfortunately, respect for the profession has undeniably dwindled in recent years. If everyone showed the reverence for teachers that my mum showed my childhood educators, then my job would be a good deal easier. However, parents like my mother are, unfortunately, becoming more scarce. Instead of valuable pillars of society, teachers are now being made to be the scapegoat and treated as babysitters. The pandemic didn't help, of course. I cried for hours at home, while newspapers blasted teachers for 'not being heroes' and keeping schools open when, in fact, we were in schools, which remained open for key worker children. I was terrified at the time due to what I'll describe as a 'colourful' medical history, but many parents still berated me for not having all of the children in. This lack of respect and understanding is undoubtedly contributing to the rising anxiety and depression among school staff. It hurts to give so much to your job only to be told, on a fairly regular basis, that it isn't enough. So this is where self-respect comes in. You have to know that you are enough. No matter what anyone else says – you *are* enough. More than enough, if you're anything like most of the teachers I have met. All you need to do to be 'enough' as a teacher is to do three things:

1. Care
2. Commit
3. Compromise

To care about the children is key. Without this compassion, why are you even here? To commit to teaching is a touch more complicated, but essentially, I mean you need to try your best, every day, whatever that looks like. It doesn't mean running yourself ragged or putting yourself second, but it does mean not just doing the bare minimum. There's a healthy place in between. Compromise is an interesting one, but I think it comes into play fairly often in schools. Children and schools themselves are ever-changing, and you need to roll with it. Things may come in that you don't like, but if you resist every change, you're going to have an awful time. You might be teaching a lesson that none of the children can understand as you'd hoped – you need to adapt it on the fly. Compromise is my catch-all term here for making changes when needed to suit the children, your colleagues, or the school as a whole. Of course, this is a huge generalisation and not at all what's written in your contract, but my point is this - you don't need to complete every piece of paperwork on time to be *enough* as a teacher. You don't need to meet the data goals - as long as you try, that's enough. Respect yourself enough to know that, yes, you are doing a good job, no matter what anyone else says.

So you're in this special club of people that increasingly few people understand or respect - what now? Well, first of all, look in the mirror and tell yourself you're a damn super-hero because that's a fact. Others may not see it, but we know it's true. Secondly, be specific with the children about what presents you want at the end of the year. That was partly a joke but partly to remind you not to feel guilty about the presents. Yes, you're 'just doing your job', but teaching is so much more than that now, and your extra mile can correspond to a pack of Malteasers without you feeling bad about it.[1] Thirdly, find the magic moments.

For example, picture this, I've got a new job at a new school. I'm an experienced teacher, but there are high expectations of me. The first half term was a long seven weeks, half term felt like a blur, and then it happened. I finally caught COVID. In retrospect, this was the perfect time. I had been working myself stupid trying to prove myself in a new setting (read: maternity contract), and I was on the verge of burning out. It was largely my own fault, I must say, as I hold myself to impossibly high standards that I have no hope of meeting (I really need to take my own advice, don't I?). So after my positive test, I was forced to stay at home and, thankfully, felt a lot more reassured than I would have been previously due to my three vaccines (thank you, NHS!) With what started as a mild cold, I sat on the sofa and got as much work done as possible. Once I had done all of the planning, preparation, and assessment I could possibly do from home, I thought to myself, why not pop in online and see how my class are doing? They were four and five, after all, and many of them had attachment issues. We had been told that we could 'remote in' if we were feeling well enough, although nobody had yet. But I thought reading a couple of stories was something that wouldn't be too difficult to do from the sofa. So after complications with technology and a very helpful member of SLT helped me out at the school's end, I was able to pop up on their screen.

That was my magic moment

Their faces lit up as though I was a bag of sweets, and that was the moment I remembered why I loved this job. I'd nearly forgotten again, in my desperate quest to prove myself, but their little faces instantly reminded me. I felt such a high just from interacting with them - and that's the thing. If teaching were just hanging out with children all day and looking after them - well, we wouldn't have the retention problem we're having. They're just full of pure joy to see you each day, and to find that moment was such a gift. I almost didn't want to leave at the end of the call, but there is only so much you can teach reception-age children through a screen - you try delivering a practical maths lesson through a whiteboard! It is vital to find those moments in teaching. It's usually the quiet times when you're sitting with a child who shares something special or a group of children catch you off guard with a funny game they're playing - it could be anything. But find those moments and cherish them, because you're going to need them.

Another friend, a teacher grappling with a challenging student and escalating behavioural issues, encountered an entirely different kind of gift. Following a meeting where concerns about the child's conduct were discussed, the parent handed over an envelope containing cash. The unsolicited offering was meant to soften the impact of the difficult conversation, raising questions about the appropriateness of such gestures. The teacher found herself at a crossroads, unsure whether to accept the money or to maintain a strict separation between professional duties and personal benefits. While acknowledging the parent's attempt to address the issues at hand, she ultimately decided to decline the cash, emphasising the importance of addressing behavioural concerns through open communication and collaboration rather than financial transactions. There are now rules in place which forbid teachers from accepting cash or, in some cases, gifts above a certain value.

These instances highlight the complexity of receiving gifts in the teaching profession. While small, thoughtful tokens of appreciation are generally well-received, larger or more extravagant gifts can blur the lines between professional duty and personal favour. Teachers, bound by a commitment to the well-being of their students and the integrity of their profession, must navigate these situations with grace and discernment. As the saying goes, it's the thought that counts, but sometimes, the thought behind a gift can inadvertently create moral quandaries for educators. Navigating these scenarios requires a delicate balance between expressing gratitude for the sentiment and upholding the ethical standards that guide the teaching profession.

Note

1 Gift-giving among parents and students can be a thoughtful gesture, a token of appreciation for the hard work and dedication teachers invest in shaping young minds. However, as the range of gifts varies, so does the potential for awkward and even inappropriate offerings. One teaching assistant found herself on the receiving end of an unexpected and perhaps unwarranted gift. In an attempt to bend the rules and expedite her child's return to school after an illness, a parent presented her with a £25 coffee voucher. The intention was clear, a subtle bribe to overlook the mandatory 48-hour window after sickness. Staring at the voucher, she found herself torn between gratitude for the gesture and the ethical dilemma it presented. While appreciating the parent's concern for their child's education, she couldn't compromise the health and well-being of the entire class by bending the rules. It was a situation that underscored the delicate balance teachers often navigate between maintaining professional boundaries and acknowledging the genuine intentions behind such gifts.

Lesson 2   Finding a purpose

Lesson objective: To find a purpose, large or small, to distract from the daily grind.

Steps to success:

- Think of your skills
- Decide how they can be applied to your situation
- Make time for yourself
- Give yourself a challenge

While teaching in itself is, of course, a noble purpose, it can become repetitive, even with the variable little factors that are children. We can find ourselves dreading Mondays and longing for Fridays week after week, while simultaneously counting down to the next school holidays (seven weeks is too long for a half term and eight is just absurd). To break this monotony, it's important to find a purpose. Now, this could be anything, depending on your skill set and the time you have available. Maybe you enjoy playing sports outside of school or can speak multiple languages. Perhaps you enjoy building Lego in your spare time or are a passionate cook – it doesn't have to be anything objectively impressive, just something you enjoy. For me, my passions lie in music, so I like to write songs for the school and come up with new initiatives to expose our pupils to music. I also love putting on a good show now and then, as well as running a choir. These things give me positive goals to work towards, as well as offering me provable, tangible progress and a sense of achievement. Taking something I love and sharing it with the children is also immensely rewarding – you might not care to hear 20 children singing Disney songs slightly out of key, but for some reason it makes my heart sing. Not everyone has time to run a club or come up with new initiatives, but the world is your oyster here. For example, you could do any of the following:

- Ask one of your children with English as an additional language to teach you one new word each day. I learned a decent amount of Russian from an adorable and hilarious little boy at my last school, which has come in useful at times. Спасибо Bogdan!
- Use your music lessons to learn an instrument with your children – in my last school, I brought in ukulele lessons for the Year 3 children, and the teachers enjoyed learning alongside the children.

DOI: 10.4324/9781003506911-3

- Start a club or occasional group doing something you're passionate about – for example, my friend (also a teacher) wants to start a Dungeons and Dragons club at her school. You may laugh, but it somehow motivated her most reluctant writer to get down 11 sentences in an hour – a personal record – all about his D&D character Florg and adventures in Pig Town.
- Start a regular activity for the staff doing something you enjoy, such as pilates or puzzles. I'd prefer puzzles, but that's a personal preference.
- Get your creative juices flowing and redesign a display/area of your classroom to be just how you want it. A colleague of mine has a rather fetching superhero-themed reading corner.

You can probably think of more tailored purposes to match your own interests, but feel free to try one of the above if you don't find them too patronising. The key is to find something that actively takes you away from the monotony of the daily grind and turns 'just another day' into something memorable and fun. My favourite part of teaching is always the happy times I spend with the children. Granted, those times can be few and far between, especially during S.A.T. season, but they're important to create. For example, one unexpected wet playtime, I introduced my class to one of my favourite childhood shows, *The Moomins*. They became so enthralled with the stories that I ended up writing an entire topic based on them. I made Moomin toys out of socks. I took their messages of environmentalism and conservation and taught them to my class. As their eyes opened wide with each new tale, I relished taking them through happy memories from my own childhood.

As a childless woman in her thirties, it can often be difficult to know the current trends for young kids. Even things I thought would keep me cool for years (*Frozen*) quickly became popular before my class of 4-year-olds was even born. Time is a cruel mistress. Luckily, the recent release of *Encanto* has got me right back to a place where I can sing a chorus and they're all engaged (it may surprise you to know that it's not actually that blasted Bruno song that's the most popular – 'Surface Pressure' is their unrivalled favourite). For those moments though, singing together on the playground or talking to the children in my choir about the finer plot points of their favourite movie, keeping up with these trends is undeniably worth it. No, I will never watch *Peppa Pig* – I can't do it and you can't make me. I've always been a Disney girl, though, so that was my way in. Your way in can be whatever you want it to be. Maybe you used to collect PokÈmon cards and your class has recently developed an interest in the new game. Perhaps you got a new puppy and that's all they want to talk about – go with it! I know a lot of adults grew up, like me, playing video games. Some people are a little embarrassed to share that at work, but you will not believe the level of respect I get from the boys in my class just for understanding the concept of Minecraft. You can enjoy these childish things because it's a wonderful way to bond with your pupils. Don't fight it!

Bringing your own passion into the classroom is also a great way to build rapport with your class. For example, the Wordle craze is going strong at the moment. For the uninitiated, it's an online word game where you get six attempts to guess the word of the day. When a letter is in the right place, it turns green. A correct letter in the wrong place turns yellow. We have a family WhatsApp group where we post our daily scores, and I can hear you rolling your eyes at that, but there are certainly far more toxic family habits than this. Anyway, my friend teaches

8-year-olds, so she thought this would be a great way to teach them some dictionary skills. They started playing it at school each day, and the response was overwhelming. They became so engaged with the game that they went back and played the previous days' Wordle games in Golden Time![1] As previously mentioned, she also took her love of the game Dungeons and Dragons into her English lessons to great success. The writing they produced was excellent, and her relationship with the children only grew as they enjoyed a new hobby together. Teaching in the early years, I have to be a little more creative. Many games I enjoy are too complicated for the four and 5-year-olds in my care, but that's where my love of music comes in. Songs are a wonderful way to teach children, and singing together can be a wonderful experience. I'm sure we all know a 'phonics song' of the classic alphabet tune. It doesn't need to be as simple as this, but it's a way to vary up your inputs that I highly recommend.

Many teachers often feel, I believe unjustly, that they need to keep themselves closed off from their pupils. Hiding in the shadows, they keep their private lives exactly that – which is, of course, fair enough if a personal choice. Sharing my little family with my class has been a gift though. All they want to talk about much of the time is their family and pets, and so sharing my life with them makes them feel closer to me. My class are absolutely fascinated by my pet tortoise and enjoy the weekly photos of him chomping on a dandelion or climbing his enclosure. Even though they insist on referring to him as a turtle, poor chap.

Now, do you remember our chat about mood hoovers? Yes, well, a common symptom of mood hoovering is the familiar 'I hate dressing up' or 'You won't catch me dead doing a fun run'. Of course, I appreciate that for some of us (me included), running is a blissful memory at this point. But take it from someone who has never been sporty but now *cannot* physically run. If you can do it – do it. Back when I was slow but capable of doing so, running (more jogging, really) a fun run with my class was actually brilliant fun. I refused at first, knowing I wouldn't be very quick or indeed graceful, but the children were (as they always are) incredibly supportive and sweet with cries of 'Go, Mrs Boucher!' and honestly the ego boost was terrific. We have a fun run scheduled today, and I'm honestly devastated that recent medical issues mean I cannot participate.

The question of dressing up is another kettle of fish entirely, but honestly, we as adults rarely get the opportunity for this silliness or reinvention. Just go with it! You don't have to go all out, spend a lot of money, or employ high production value. Just join in and I promise you the children will love it, and you'll feel more included for going along with it.

However you choose to bond with your class, this can all link back to finding your purpose. When your purpose and their passion intertwine – you've got a recipe for success.

As well as finding a purpose in work, it's important to find one outside of that. Easier said than done, however. When living with another teacher, we would regularly arrive home at around half past five and promptly fall asleep. This was both unplanned and unexpected, but not altogether unlikely. You see, nothing prepares you for the sheer exhaustion of teaching. It's demanding, it's relentless, and the expectations never remain the same for more than a day. Everyone says you need a work/life balance, but what do you do when you're just too tired to live? I'm a member of a local theatre group, and the very last thing I want to do after a staff meeting on a Monday is to go to a rehearsal that finishes less than eight hours before I have to get up for work the next day. However, I do believe it to be vital to my mental health. To have this purpose – the goal of a show to work towards – gives my life more meaning than just work.

I manage this, barely, but I manage it. Once I'm there and I'm singing and laughing, I know I've made the right choice to drag myself out of the house and see my friends. What amazes me, however, is my friends who are also teachers, also in my theatre group, and *also* … have children. To teachers with children – my fullest admiration can never be expressed enough. How do you do it? Seriously, I'm fascinated. You also give me a wonderful sense of perspective.

For these people, of course, you already have a grander purpose than I will ever have – your own children. Why not learn a new instrument with them or do an art project together? Maybe you could both learn a new word in Chinese each day or play one of those infernal word games on your phones each morning to see who can get the highest score. I don't know, I don't have children. I have a tortoise and a puppy. You're on your own here.

It is also important to keep challenging yourself; otherwise, life can get boring. Recently, I was talking with a friend who lamented the lack of 'life skill' education in schools, and it made me think. Why on earth *don't* we teach our children first aid as a matter of priority? Why do we waste time learning log rolls in PE when we could be teaching our class invaluable self-defence skills, and why, at the age of 31, do I still not have the faintest idea how taxes or pensions work? So I came upon a new personal challenge – teaching my 4-year-olds some life skills. Granted, you can't explain the finer points of National Insurance to a child who's barely toilet-trained, but what you can do is teach them the basic concepts. I decided to make a game that would (to an extremely simple level) explain to them how the system of government works.

This is how I did it:

- I made some laminated cards for public services the children would be familiar with (school, hospital, police etc.).
- I gave the children a finite amount of pretend coins (chocolate or not, it's really up to you how much you want them to care about this!).
- I told the children that they had to decide where their coins went.
- Depending on where they chose to spend their money, there were different scenarios. For example, if they spent all their money on schools, all the children got state-of-the-art computers, but the hospitals suffered and people didn't get the treatment they needed. I tried not to make this too dark, but I wanted them to understand the concept that money wasn't infinite, and difficult decisions had to be made in life, which had consequences.

It's incredibly simplistic, I know, but this led to discussions about where their parents' money goes, who gets to choose, why we can't just print money, if they can eat their chocolate coins yet, and how we decide who gets to make these choices. It's a precursor to explaining things later on that will help them navigate adult life in a way I feel I was personally never prepared for. It also gave me a purpose that, realistically, high-frequency words and capital letters do not. Don't get me wrong, they are important, but fairly dull and incredibly repetitive after ten years in teaching. Next year I plan to completely overhaul my PE lessons to focus on first aid, self-defence, and discipline. Watch this space for lesson plans!

It also helps to go in with an open mind. When Ofsted visited us, we were given a small plea to be outside at lunchtime 'just this once' to be with the children. I found myself on a bean bag in the reading area (much more my speed than running around!) and a small crowd of excited and equally uncoordinated children quickly gathered around me for story time. I ended up feeling so light after that lunch hour that I decided to make it a weekly thing – I now have lunchtime story time every Friday. Should I give up my lunch break for what is essentially 'free labour'? No, of course not, and I'm not saying you should. What I am saying, though, is that if you find something that brings you joy – don't resist it just because others might.

Dungeons, dragons, above and beyond

In the bustling halls of St Clement's Primary School, Ms Thompson navigated her way through the maze of classrooms with a purposeful stride. As a seasoned teacher, she had seen her fair share of students, each with their unique quirks and challenges. However, it was the arrival of a new student, Jake, that would prove to be a transformative experience for both teacher and pupil. Word travelled quickly around the staff that Jake was a foster child, recently transferred to St Clement's Primary School after a tumultuous past. His file was marked with incidents of disruptive behaviour and academic struggles, and concerned glances and hushed tones hoping that he wouldn't be allocated to their class. The teachers whispered in the staff room about the 'difficult' child who seemed to resist any connection attempts. The label of a troublemaker stuck to Jake like an unwanted shadow, casting him into a sea of judgment and misunderstanding. Ms Thompson, however, approached the situation with an open heart and an unwavering belief in the potential of every child. She had read Jake's file, absorbing the challenges he had faced, but instead of seeing a problem, she saw an opportunity to make a difference. As she welcomed Jake into her Year 2 class, she could sense the scepticism in the eyes of her colleagues, but she remained undeterred.

In those initial days, Jake lived up to the expectations others had set for him. He was disruptive, prone to outbursts, and detached from the class activities. Other teachers labelled him as 'naughty', dismissing any attempts to engage with him. But Ms Thompson saw beyond the behaviour, recognising a spark of curiosity in Jake's eyes, a longing for connection masked by a tough exterior. Determined to break through Jake's walls, Ms Thompson observed him closely, trying to identify any interests that could serve as a bridge. One day, while walking around the nearby supermarket, she bumped into Jake and his stepfather. She noticed that Jake was engrossed in a handheld gaming device, navigating through a virtual world with unmatched intensity. The game involved intricate battles, strategy, and a rich fantasy narrative. Seizing the opportunity, Ms Thompson struck up a conversation about the game. To her surprise, Jake's guarded demeanour softened as he animatedly spoke about his love for fighting games. Ms Thompson, recognising the potential for connection, decided to think of a way she could use this newfound knowledge to connect to the pupil.

The next day at school, Ms Thompson found Jake in the playground and proposed a unique idea – what if they created their own fantasy world and characters during lunchtime? At present, Jake was kept inside at lunchtimes anyway 'for the other children's safety' and so she wouldn't be taking away any of his time outdoors – that had already been done. Jake thought about this proposal but decided that anything would be better than sitting in a sad, empty classroom for half an hour each day, so he tentatively agreed.

Ms Thompson's classroom, over time, witnessed an unconventional alliance taking shape. Instead of sitting in isolation, Jake and Ms Thompson gathered at a corner table with sheets of paper and a collection of coloured pencils. Together, they started sketching characters inspired by Jake's favourite fighting games. Ms Thompson, an artist at heart, guided Jake through the process, offering insights and encouragement. As the fantasy world on their lunchtime canvas began to take shape, so did the bond between teacher and student. The rigid lines of teacher-student hierarchy blurred, replaced by a partnership fueled by shared creativity, though not devoid of authority or respect. The other teachers, initially sceptical of Ms Thompson's unconventional approach, watched with raised eyebrows as Jake's behaviour in class began to change.

Drawing became a gateway for Jake to express himself. The battles they sketched on paper became the foundation for epic stories that Jake started writing in a tattered notebook. The tales were filled with heroes, villains, and the intricate details of a world born from their combined imaginations. Ms Thompson marvelled at the transformation in Jake's writing – the once reluctant student now pouring his thoughts onto paper with newfound enthusiasm. The lunchtime drawing sessions became a sacred ritual for Jake and Ms Thompson. The fantasy world they created together provided an escape for Jake, a refuge from the challenges he faced. As they worked on their drawings, Ms Thompson subtly introduced elements of academic learning – maths concepts hidden in the design of characters, and vocabulary woven into the dialogue of their stories. Learning became an organic process, seamlessly integrated into their shared passion.

Word of the remarkable change in Jake's behaviour spread through the school like wildfire. Other teachers, initially dismissive of Ms Thompson's approach, now sought her guidance on connecting with their challenging students. The transformation in Jake wasn't just about academics; it was about finding common ground, about recognising the untapped potential in every child. Moreover, Ms Thompson, previously swimming through each teaching day with a familiar monotony, had discovered a wonderful new purpose, which also allowed her a creative outlet.

On a sunny afternoon, as the school year drew to a close, Ms Thompson received a heartfelt note from Jake. In his carefully written words, he expressed gratitude for seeing beyond the troubled exterior, for believing in his ability to create, and for being a friend when he needed one the most. The note ended with a promise – Jake vowed to continue writing stories, not just as an escape, but as a celebration of the fantastical world they had built together. The bond forged through shared drawings and epic stories had not only transformed Jake's academic journey but had also left an indelible mark on Ms Thompson's teaching philosophy.

Note

1 Golden Time, for the unfamiliar, is something some schools give children (and teachers) on a Friday afternoon. The children can choose what they want to do, from a selection of activities. Usually, they all choose to play outside or play games – it's a lovely time to get to know them and try out some of the previous lessons if you have the time.

Lesson 3   Prioritise

Lesson objective: To learn to put certain tasks ahead of others and to let go of those you deem unnecessary, within reason.

Steps to success:

- Do one thing at a time
- Think about who you're doing this for
- Organise yourself

Now this is an important one. During my lifetime, I must have been told to 'just say no' a thousand times or more. But I'm a people pleaser, and I just can't do it. What's more, it's rarely an option in teaching. That's why prioritising is key. It sounds simple, but rank your tasks - what's more important right now: that paperwork for Ofsted or your SEN child's intervention plan? The Ofsted paperwork might be due a day before the intervention, but what if you only have time to do one right now? What is most urgent: that dinosaur-themed display you've been meaning to do or prepping for your next lesson? I still, on occasion, find myself getting caught up with an idea and forgetting what's more immediately important. Usually, I have a great idea for an area of my classroom and end up spending my entire lunch hour moving furniture when I should be eating lunch (my resolution for this coming school year is to eat *before* any such activity, as well as to ask my stronger, less-prone-to-back-pain friends to move my furniture for me). Your priority should be, of course, things that directly benefit the children. Ofsted-related tasks should be right at the very bottom and, depending on your current state, near the top of it should be your own self-care. If you've been asked, for example, as we all have, to copy one piece of paperwork or planning document over into a largely identical but apparently 'improved' format - this can wait. Also, if you're the kind of person who can say no - let it be to nonsense like this. If, however, your next lesson starts in five minutes and you haven't yet printed the sheets - well, that's a priority. Run, do it now, go! We've all been there - and then of *course* the printer is out of paper. Take some with you - oh, you've already gone.

So out of the following tasks, how would you go about completing them? Order them from 1-10 with 1 being 'the thing I would do first'. Go ahead, I'll wait.

- Plan tomorrow's lessons
- Put up that display

DOI: 10.4324/9781003506911-4

- Input your termly data
- Complete the behaviour report for Douglas biting Sam
- Email the SENCo your concerns about Alison
- Reply to the head's email asking for 500 words about the Summer Fayre for the newsletter
- Redesign your book corner
- Tidy your classroom
- Mark the work from the last lesson

How did you do? Of course, many of these tasks depend on where you are in the term. If you've just started, for example, that data input can wait. Tomorrow's lesson, however, and your concerns about Alison are more important. Reports and paperwork can pile up, but they don't immediately benefit the children, so let those come next. It's really up to you how you go about the rest, but remember to prioritise in a way that works for you and your working life.

I would order them like this, but there's no scoring system here, so don't panic:

- Email the SENCo your concerns about Alison
- Plan tomorrow's lessons
- Complete the behaviour report for Douglas biting Sam
- Tidy your classroom
- Mark the work from the last lesson
- Input your termly data
- Reply to the head's email asking for 500 words about the Summer Fayre for the newsletter
- Put up that display
- Redesign your book corner

I tend to put immediate aesthetic tasks, such as tidying the classroom, much higher than things like displays. An untidy classroom will immediately impact the children's ability to learn, but if the display is up a week late – will it affect them? Not really. While ordering the tasks, I shuffled them around quite a few times as there are infinite options here, but my main driver was – what, if left undone, will negatively impact the children first?

Don't misconstrue this advice though – I don't mean 'leave all the paperwork until the last minute' because that will come back to bite you. I am mocked and praised in unequal measure for my organisational skills, and while it may seem easy to outsiders, it's something I had to learn (although to deny my parents' influence on this would be unfair – thanks, Mum and Dad, your anal-retentiveness is genetic!). However, my first year of teaching was not so organised. I felt like I was on a constant treadmill, running to keep up with every demand. Over time, however, I learned to stay ahead of the game rather than behind it. If there's something I *could* be doing, and I have the mental space to do it at that time, I'd rather get it out of the way than leave it for tomorrow. At the end of each day, if I ever find myself unexpectedly finished early, I always think of something I can take away from my 'tomorrow self'. What could I do today that will save me a job tomorrow? This isn't always possible, and I still get swamped at times, but to go in with an organised intention is certainly helpful in a job where the tasks are never-ending. And that doesn't just mean buying a pretty diary. Take it from someone with several beautiful but empty diaries. I've found the most effective way for me to stay organised is Post-its on my PC. They're easy to jot down in the moment, I see them all the time, and once I've completed them, I can scrunch them up into a satisfying little ball of completion. Find what works for you – maybe you're a 'write it on your hand' person or even an Excel spreadsheet person – there's no judgment. Everyone organises themselves differently, the important thing is to *try* to be organised.

What's more, try to pause with each task's completion, to just take a moment to reflect on your accomplishment. It won't take long, but it will make a big difference. If you ever sat down to think about how much you do in a single day, you'd be amazed. We are so used to ignoring this fact, however, and living with the feeling that we've hardly done anything at all as there is always so much more to be done. This brings me to my next point – you will never be done. It's not about crossing things off a list because the list will never end. That's why it's so important to look around and notice the benefits of what you're doing. Finished a lesson plan? Look at your class enjoying your lesson – Sarah is really getting into that counting resource you made – good for you! Completed all your data? Marvel at the upward trajectory (while tactfully ignoring the unrealistic targets you've probably been given). Finished your display? Take a photo and chuck it on Pinterest, it looks stunning.

But don't just take my word for it – there's a huge amount of research to back this up. Prioritising tasks is a fundamental skill that plays a crucial role in maintaining a healthy work-life balance, especially in demanding professions such as teaching. As educators face myriad responsibilities, ranging from lesson planning to administrative paperwork, the ability to discern and prioritise tasks becomes paramount. Scientific research underscores the significance of effective prioritisation in fostering a more manageable and fulfilling work-life equilibrium for teachers.

Numerous studies in organisational psychology and occupational health emphasise the impact of workload and time management on overall job satisfaction and well-being. A study conducted by Grant et al. (2017) explored the relationship between workload, time management behaviours, and job satisfaction among teachers. The findings revealed that teachers who employed effective time management strategies reported higher levels of job satisfaction and reduced stress levels. Prioritising tasks emerged as a central aspect of these time management behaviours, allowing educators to focus on essential responsibilities and allocate resources efficiently.

Additionally, a comprehensive review by Skaalvik and Skaalvik (2017) delved into the various factors influencing teacher job satisfaction and well-being. The review highlighted the role of autonomy and control over one's work environment as critical contributors to teachers' overall job satisfaction. Prioritisation of tasks provides teachers with a sense of control, enabling them to make informed decisions about how to allocate their time and resources. This control, in turn, positively influences job satisfaction and contributes to a healthier work-life balance.

The concept of cognitive fatigue, a state characterised by mental exhaustion and reduced cognitive performance, is also pertinent to the discussion. Multiple studies, including research by Van Hooff et al. (2005), emphasise the cognitive demands placed on teachers, particularly in managing multiple tasks simultaneously. Prioritising tasks helps mitigate cognitive fatigue by allowing educators to focus on one task at a time, enhancing their cognitive resources and reducing the mental strain associated with multitasking. Moreover, the impact of prioritisation extends beyond individual well-being and job satisfaction; it also influences student outcomes. A study by Hattie (2009) highlighted the factors that significantly contribute to student achievement. Notably, teacher effectiveness emerged as a crucial factor, and effective time management and task prioritisation are integral components of effective teaching. When teachers allocate their time strategically, focusing on high-priority tasks such as lesson planning and student engagement, it positively influences the learning environment and, consequently, student outcomes.

The practical implementation of prioritisation strategies aligns with the broader framework of time management principles. Research by Macan et al. (1990) emphasised the importance of goal-setting, planning, and prioritising tasks in effective time management. These principles not only enhance individual performance but also contribute to a more balanced and sustainable approach to work.

In conclusion, scientific research illuminates the significance of prioritisation in the context of teaching and its impact on work-life balance. Teachers who effectively prioritise tasks experience higher levels of job satisfaction, reduced stress, and improved overall well-being. Moreover, the positive outcomes extend to the classroom environment, influencing student achievement and engagement. As educators navigate the multifaceted demands of their profession, the skill of prioritisation emerges as a valuable tool for creating a more harmonious and fulfilling work-life balance.

Sources for this chapter

Grant, A. M., Dweck, C. S., & O'Brien, L. (2017). Teacher burnout and the role of goals: A motivational perspective. In *Handbook of Human Motivation* (pp.†501–515). Academic Press.

Hattie, J. (2009). *Visible Learning: A Synthesis of Over 800 Meta-Analyses Relating to Achievement*. Routledge.

Macan, T. H., Shahani, C., Dipboye, R. L., & Phillips, A. P. (1990). College students' time management: Correlations with academic performance and stress. *Journal of Educational Psychology*, 82(3), 405.

Skaalvik, E. M., & Skaalvik, S. (2017). Dimensions of teacher burnout: Relations with potential stressors at school. In *Handbook of Stress in the Occupations* (pp.†311–324). Edward Elgar Publishing.

Van Hooff, M. L., Geurts, S. A., Taris, T. W., Kompier, M. A., Dikkers, J. S., & Houtman, I. L. (2005). Disentangling the causal relationships between work-home interference and employee health. *Scandinavian Journal of Work, Environment & Health*, 29(3), 213–223.

Lesson 4 Self-care

Lesson objective: To learn to prioritise yourself above other things (see Lesson 3).

Steps to success:

- Value yourself and your time
- Don't overstretch yourself
- Don't feel pressured to 'be happy' – it's deeper than that

One of the more frustrating trends I've seen in recent years can be summed up in a recent quote I read from a friend:

> We can't have unrealistic expectations for educators and then gaslight them by saying they need to practise self-care.

We are not stressed because we're not looking after ourselves. We are stressed because the job *is* stressful. There have been various methods schools have used to encourage teacher happiness lately ranging from banning negative talk in staff rooms (yes, seriously) to positive posters on the walls. Better approaches I've seen have included well-being baskets in the staff room and offers of extra PPA time for those feeling snowed under. The problem with this is that the job cannot be changed. Not at a school level, at least. They can try and decrease our stress levels, but unless they can decrease the expectations on us (unlikely), then it can be a bit of a lost cause. So of course, much like everything else, it falls on us to improve our self-care. The first step is to value yourself as a person, not just as an educator. It does not define you, and while it takes a large part of your time, you are entitled to live a life outside of that. If you're finding yourself completely rammed with schoolwork, timetable in some time where you ban yourself from working or even thinking about work. That may sound silly, but it's difficult for some people just to switch off. I hear the voices of 'What if that means I miss a deadline?' If you are so busy with work that you can't give yourself half an hour each day just to exist (children of your own aside!), then you're working much, much too hard. Perhaps look at Lesson 3 for some tips on that.

One of the most difficult things about teaching is that it is a job you are expected to take home with you, even though you're not realistically paid to do so. It's less explicit in your contract and more of an unwritten rule of the profession. You have to create your own boundaries here. I have strong feelings about my home being my personal space, and where possible,

DOI: 10.4324/9781003506911-5

I prefer to stay at school late to mark my books so that once I get home – I'm done. Easy to say as a reception teacher, I agree, but I've taught older children as well and just about managed this. Once in a while, I would have to bring some books home, but it always seemed to take longer and made me feel dejected. This all depends, of course, on your home life. I know some teachers with children who need to be home for them by a certain time, as well as those who stay late as they find it easier to get work done without having to care for their children at the same time, like a multitalented juggler.

Overstretching yourself can be incredibly easy as a teacher – all you have to do is say yes, to everything – like a brittle rubber band crying in the cupboard as you're stretched 11 different ways simultaneously. While choosing not to do something you've been asked may make you feel like a failure, you have to remember that you're not your best self or the best teacher you can be when you're feeling overwhelmed. Human beings are prone to irritability and impatience when under stress, which, as we know, is not conducive to an environment where children can learn. Putting some things on the back burner isn't necessarily failing, but often, it's making the smart choice for yourself and your pupils. Further, pupils' well-being can tie in closely with your own. Consider the following: does it ever seem as though the children's behaviour is worse when you're having a bad day? It's probably because it is. When you're feeling awful, they can tell and will sometimes act accordingly, depending on their grasp of human emotions. A calm and happy teacher, even one who is pretending to some extent, can command a class far easier than one who is emotional and shouting.

'But we're human!' I hear you shout. Yes, tell me about it. I have bad days – some especially awful – but the thing is, letting it take me over at work is a guaranteed way to make it worse. When I'm feeling depressed, the best place for me to be is in class. Somehow, when I see their little faces, it goes away. Not permanently or completely, but at that moment, maybe because I know I *can't* show it, or because I know how much they need me to be strong, it's easier to subdue. The fact is, these children look to you to show them how to regulate emotions, especially those whose parents are unable to. It's an enormous responsibility, but there are things you can do to work on both your emotional state and the children's at the same time.

I would like to take a moment now to discuss something I have struggled with throughout my career. It is something unspoken, something frowned upon, and something hidden away whenever possible. The recent news of teacher suicides due to Ofsted and other pressures is nothing new. Mental health among teachers is variable, but many of us suffer from depression, anxiety, and other difficulties we must struggle through daily. I vividly remember my first day at my very first school as a qualified teacher. I received a concerned phone call from HR, asking me if I was 'safe to teach' with my 'mental health issues'. This question has come up time and again, and each time it does, it hits me like a boulder. I think it is the implication that I as a person would be unsafe to be around children that hurts the most. In my decade of teaching, I have never let my illnesses show to my pupils, and many teachers, who are not diagnosed with mental health differences, have been found time and again crying in cupboards, understandably. So why is the implication still there? I cannot tell you how much it hurt when, recently, after a particularly difficult time, I was asked whether I was 'fit for work'. Now, I understand that in the depths of a breakdown, perhaps one isn't quite able to give their best. However, put me in front of a class of children, and I can do anything. And because of my history, I feel constant pressure to be even more emotionally regulated in class than my colleagues. I feel an enormous responsibility to teach my pupils the emotional regulation and calming techniques that would have helped me growing up, and I truly believe that my trauma has enabled me to get through to several children from difficult backgrounds with whom other adults were unable to empathise and connect. This paragraph may not have applied to you, but I would like you to consider, for a moment, how you can support a positive change to reduce the 'othering' of professionals with mental health issues. It is an unwelcome additional obstacle that many of us face daily.

Something I like to do with my class that helps them as well as me is mindfulness. As a music specialist, I always veer towards the musical route with this and made a little 'Music & Mindfulness' PowerPoint. We put it on in the mornings, after break times, and whenever else they need to calm down. We select the music or soundscape we want to listen to, close our eyes, and focus on our breathing. It takes minutes, but trust me, it's effective. The adults need to do it as well – it may be tempting to use those two extra minutes to prep while the children are occupied – but ultimately it's great for your well-being too. My teaching assistant adores it! We also love a good 'brain break'. Singing, dancing – any kind of movement, really – can all aid the children's concentration and break up a challenging lesson. In a world where we are always so busy, we must give our children the tools to cope with that hecticness as they grow. With a new focus on emotional self-regulation in early years settings, there's never been a better time to equip pupils with these skills.

Some other ideas for easy mindful time:

- Ask the children to find and name silently
  o Five things they can see
  o Four things they can hear
  o Three things they can smell
  o Two things they can touch
  o One thing they can taste (tell them not to lick each other)
- Simply ask – 'Close your eyes and listen for sounds.'
- Naming one thing they can see for each colour of the rainbow (purple is surprisingly challenging!)
- Asking them to create a made-up character in their head and have a conversation with them about their current thoughts and worries
- Place your hands on your chest and stomach (above the diaphragm) and take deep breaths
- Breathing techniques such as square breathing (breathe in for four seconds, out for four seconds, and repeat, imagining you are going around the sides of a square)
- Ask the children what they are grateful for/made them smile today

Happier children make for happier adults. I always try to decrease the pressure on my pupils whenever possible, as their frustrations inevitably come my way if I don't. But what about us? Well, every little helps, or so I hear, and so here are some ideas for boosting your self-care in the workplace:

- Cake (okay, that was too easy)
- Start a staff social club, for example, games in the staff room on Fridays or yoga at lunch on Wednesday – your initial response will be 'Who has time!?' but you'll be glad you did

- Make yourself a treat basket for emergencies with your favourite things (fancy tea, Pringles, whatever you're into!)
- Make a gratitude board and anonymously put up thank yous to fellow staff members for the inevitable help they give you each week (just make sure you don't leave people out!)
- Make a 'Kids say the funniest things' board in the staff room (it's what it sounds like)
- Have a board divided into two – on one side, write your name if you inexplicably have some extra time or want to give someone a hand; on the other side, write your name if you're snowed under. Pair up and help each other out. (Note: SLT should be encouraged to write their names on the former side whenever possible!)
- I can't overstate this one enough: TAKE. YOUR. LUNCH. BREAK
- At least a 20 minutes. It *does* make a difference. (Later note: As I edit this chapter late on a Thursday evening, I chide myself for not taking any kind of lunch break today, but it's report writing season, what do you expect?)
- Listen to music while you work before/after school (my colleague had 'Hits from the 80s' blasting out the other morning and *everyone* felt better for it)

The list is endless, of course, but the most important thing to note is to permit yourself to do *something* to take better care of yourself at work. I know you don't want to, and I know it feels selfish, but *you* know you're better for those children when you're in a good place mentally.

Scientifically speaking, in the current landscape of education, the demand for effective teaching is heightened by an array of factors, including evolving curricula, diverse student needs, and the ever-changing dynamics of the educational environment. As teachers navigate through these challenges, the importance of self-care has garnered increased attention in both academic and professional spheres. Scientific evidence underscores the critical role of self-care in promoting teacher well-being, enhancing job satisfaction, and somewhat idealistically, contributing to the overall success of the educational system.

The neurobiology of stress

Research in neurobiology provides insights into the impact of stress on the brain and its implications for educators. Chronic stress, often associated with the teaching profession, can lead to adverse effects on cognitive functions, emotional regulation, and overall mental health. The amygdala, a key brain region involved in processing emotions, tends to become hyperactive under prolonged stress, contributing to heightened emotional responses and potential burn-out. Moreover, the prefrontal cortex, responsible for decision-making and impulse control, may experience reduced functionality, impairing a teacher's ability to manage classroom challenges effectively. This is often colloquially referred to as 'brain fog' and can be summed up by my poor performance at story time the other day when despite my very best efforts to read *The Three Little Pigs* to my class (they always choose that one because I do funny voices), I just couldn't get my words out. It was reviewed poorly by a very critical 4-year-old, I can tell you.

Scientific studies, such as those conducted by McEwen and Morrison (2013) in the field of neuroscience, emphasise the need for proactive stress management strategies to mitigate the negative consequences of this chronic stress. Self-care practices, ranging from mindfulness exercises to leisure activities, have demonstrated the potential to modulate stress responses, promoting neural plasticity and resilience in the face of professional demands. It was this research that resonated with me most. Taking a break a few times a day to do some breathing just isn't enough – my brain has been wired, for so many years, to panic and dwell on the negatives. Neural plasticity implies that this can be changed, albeit with a great deal of personal work, and this gave me hope.

Psychological perspectives on teacher well-being

From a psychological standpoint, the connection between teacher well-being and effective job performance is well-established. Numerous studies, including those by Skaalvik and Skaalvik (2017), have identified a reciprocal relationship between teacher well-being and instructional quality. Positive teacher well-being is associated with greater enthusiasm, commitment to teaching, and a nurturing classroom environment, fostering optimal conditions for student learning. While this may sound patronising (as I certainly felt it did during my PGCE when we studied this research), it is unavoidably accurate. Conversely, neglecting self-care can lead to burn-out, emotional exhaustion, and reduced job satisfaction. The transactional model of stress and coping (Lazarus & Folkman, 1984) highlights the dynamic interplay between stressors, coping strategies, and the subjective appraisal of well-being. Teachers who engage in effective self-care practices are better equipped to cope with stressors, preventing the escalation of negative emotional states and maintaining a more positive appraisal of their professional roles.

Social dynamics and support systems

The social dimension of self-care cannot be overlooked, as the teaching profession often involves collaboration and interconnectedness among educators. Social support has been identified as a crucial buffer against the detrimental effects of stress (Cohen & Wills, 1985). The creation of staff social clubs and gratitude boards, as previously suggested, aligns with social support frameworks that contribute to fostering a positive and supportive workplace culture. Furthermore, empirical evidence, such as the findings from studies by O'Connor et al. (2010), emphasises the role of positive workplace relationships in promoting teacher well-being and job satisfaction. Collaborative initiatives, where teachers can share ideas, provide mutual assistance, and celebrate each other's successes, contribute to the development of a resilient and supportive professional community. My greatest enjoyment at work, after the children, is always from moments with colleagues I can consider my friends.

Economic and policy perspectives

Beyond the micro level dynamics of teaching environments, macro level factors, including economic considerations and educational policies, further underscore the need for comprehensive self-care strategies. Educational reforms and policy changes often introduce new challenges and expectations for teachers. The pressure to meet performance metrics, adhere to standardised testing requirements, and adapt to evolving pedagogical approaches can contribute to heightened stress levels, as we well know.

Economic pressures, such as budget constraints and resource limitations, may exacerbate the challenges faced by educators. It is within this context that self-care initiatives become imperative not only for individual well-being but also for sustaining the effectiveness and resilience of the teaching workforce. Research by Ingersoll and Strong (2011) highlights the correlation between teacher retention and job satisfaction, emphasising the economic implications of addressing teacher well-being to ensure a stable and proficient teaching workforce. This raises a crucial point for our leaders – if teacher retention is such an issue due to low job satisfaction, why is it still delegated to us to solve that problem by simply 'being happier'? I do hope that leadership teams learn from this research that the facade of happiness and a couple of self-care posters just isn't enough to mitigate the crisis we are facing in this sector.

Cultural and ethical considerations

The cultural and ethical dimensions of self-care in teaching encompass the recognition of diverse needs and identities within the profession. Culturally responsive self-care practices acknowledge the unique challenges faced by educators from different cultural backgrounds, contributing to a more inclusive and equitable work environment. Ethical considerations underscore the responsibility of educational institutions to prioritise the well-being of their teaching staff, recognising the reciprocal impact on student outcomes. Educational ethics, as discussed by Strike (2018), involve a commitment to fostering a positive and supportive educational community that values the holistic well-being of its members. From a cultural competence perspective, self-care practices should be culturally sensitive and respectful of the diverse identities present in the teaching profession. Age can come into this as well, as older members of staff often report feeling isolated and 'pushed out' in favour of younger, 'fresher' teachers. I discuss the pitfalls of this later on, but do look out for your more experienced members of staff and, importantly, value them.

The intersectionality of self-care and professional development

The integration of self-care practices into the realm of professional development signifies a paradigm shift in understanding teaching as a holistic and sustainable profession. The traditional model of professional development often emphasises skill acquisition, curriculum knowledge, and pedagogical techniques. However, the contemporary landscape recognises the interconnectedness of personal well-being and professional efficacy.

Scientific literature, such as the work by Darling-Hammond and Richardson (2009), advocates for a comprehensive approach to teacher development that includes the cultivation of emotional intelligence, stress management skills, and self-reflective practices. The integration of self-care within the framework of professional development aligns with the concept of the teacher as a lifelong learner, not only in subject matter expertise but also in emotional intelligence and well-being. By bringing these lessons into teacher training, in a practical way (as opposed to merely theoretical, academic research), teachers can be better prepared for the challenges before them.

In conclusion, the scientific evidence presented underscores the urgency and significance of prioritising self-care in the teaching profession. From neurobiological responses to stress and psychological dimensions of well-being to social, economic, and cultural considerations, the multifaceted nature of self-care aligns with the complex demands of contemporary education. It cannot merely be a tokenistic endeavour but a foundational element that sustains both individual educators and the integrity of the educational system as a whole. Recognising and valuing self-care should not be seen as a personal indulgence but a strategic imperative for creating a resilient, motivated, and effective teaching workforce capable of meeting the challenges of the twenty-first century educational landscape.

Sources for this chapter

Cohen, S., & Wills, T. A. (1985). Stress, social support, and the buffering hypothesis. *Psychological Bulletin*, 98(2), 310-357. https://doi.org/10.1037/0033-2909.98.2.310

Darling-Hammond, L., & Richardson, N. (2009). Teacher learning: What matters? *Educational Leadership*, 66(5), 46-53. https://www.ascd.org/el/articles/teacher-learning-what-matters

Ingersoll, R. M., & Strong, M. (2011). The impact of induction and mentoring programs for beginning teachers: A critical review of the research. *Review of Educational Research*, 81(2), 201-233. https://doi.org/10.3102/0034654311403323

Lazarus, R. S., & Folkman, S. (1984). *Stress, Appraisal, and Coping*. Springer Publishing Company.

McEwen, B. S., & Morrison, J. H. (2013). The brain on stress: Vulnerability and plasticity of the prefrontal cortex over the life course. *Neuron*, 79(1), 16-29. https://doi.org/10.1016/j.neuron.2013.06.028

O'Connor, R., Mueller, J., & Hmieleski, K. M. (2010). Corporate entrepreneurship: A review and future research agenda. *Journal of Business Venturing*, 25(5), 500-510.

Skaalvik, E. M., & Skaalvik, S. (2017). Still motivated to teach? A study of school context variables, stress and job satisfaction among teachers in senior high school. *Social Psychology of Education*, 20(1), 15-37. https://doi.org/10.1007/s11218-016-9363-9

Strike, K. A. (2018). Ethics and education: An overview. In E. N. Zalta (Ed.), *The Stanford Encyclopedia of Philosophy* (Winter 2018 Edition). Metaphysics Research Lab, Stanford University. https://plato.stanford.edu/archives/win2018/entries/ethics-education/

Lesson 5   Managing your inner mood hoover

Lesson objective: To limit the amount of negativity presented in the workplace.

Steps to success:

* No more 'and another thing ...'
* Be self-aware
* It's not about 'just being happy'

'Mood Hoover' is an unusual phrase, I grant you. Once, at an academy-wide Inset day, we had a motivational speaker as a guest. He spoke to us for four and a half hours about how our positivity is our responsibility. This chapter is not about that. As I mentioned in previous chapters, gaslighting teachers by working them to death and then blaming them for their own unhappiness is not the way to go. This speaker, however well-meaning, was fairly divisive within my particular group. He endearingly referred to the more negative people amongst us as the aforementioned 'mood hoovers', and of course, that went down very poorly with those he was clearly targeting. A defensive hush bristled around the room, and from that point on, many ears were closed to any advice he might have to offer. Some of the advice was sound and well-researched. Some of it was generic, clichÈd, and clumsily applied to education. Overall, though, the people he was targeting were not the people most receptive to it. I found myself at that moment wondering, 'Am I one of those people?' In teaching, it is virtually impossible to remain positive all of the time. You're frequently berated and overworked, and so, yes, the staff room becomes a sort of venting space. Some schools have gone so far as to ban negative talk altogether and, in doing so, demonise the staff and ignore the root of the problem. Stopping the negativity won't fix it, however. It will still be there, and resentment will undoubtedly follow, as it did with the poor man tasked with cheering up our academy staff. The only real way of turning negativity into positivity is by acknowledging it. The following conversation will probably be familiar to many of you.

Sally:	Those kids are 'on one' today. I don't know if it's the weather but ...
Chloe:	Oh, I know. And did you hear SLT whisper the 'O' word this morning?
Jenny:	And I heard they might lay off the teaching assistants because the academy is top-slicing our budgets!

DOI: 10.4324/9781003506911-6

This is the familiar yet inevitable 'and another thing' of being a primary school teacher. Because there will always be another thing to complain about. It is important, however, to break that cycle. Now read the following exchange:

Sally:	Those kids are on one today. I don't know if it's the weather but …
Chloe:	Sally, I hear you, those children have been off the wall today! What have you got planned for your weekend?

The problem is still there. The problem, realistically, cannot be fixed. Sally just wants to be heard and acknowledged. Many of us then fall into the trap of a negative cycle – 'and another thing!' – which only fuels everyone's bad mood. Sharing and venting are important, but the key is to know when to turn that around, draw a line under it, and choose to talk about something positive. You owe it to yourselves and you owe it to each other to allow yourselves to be hopeful. Not because someone told you to or because 'negativity is bad' – it isn't; it's sometimes a necessary coping mechanism – but because you deserve happiness. Let that sink in for a moment.

Now onto the conspiracy theories. Budgets being syphoned off to academy higher-ups (this does happen, unfortunately); shady ways of using money earmarked for children with special educational needs; secret affairs within management; the office staff leaving early – I've heard a lot of bizarre and, sometimes accurate, conspiracy theories in schools. They can help bind colleagues together against a common goal, but they can also damage a workplace. It's important to be able to discern the facts from fiction. Of course, if anything genuinely dodgy is going on in your workplace, it needs to be addressed and resolved. Just don't get too carried away at the expense of your relationships with your co-workers, or you'll likely learn the hard way, trust me.

Moving on from 'mood hoovers' now, but not a million miles away. We turn, instead, to Mona. Mona has been teaching since 'before you were born, son', and she's 'been at this school for thirty years'. Mona is a legend. Mona is a hero. Mona is a mood hoover. It's easy to roll your eyes at the Monas because they often moan about 'this new thing' or 'that new thing' and can be resistant to change. However, Mona has seen her job lose respect, and value, all while gaining workload over the years, and to be honest, if I were Mona, I'd be cross too. It can be frustrating to have a member of staff who 'refuses to get with the times' but then, she's seen it all before. Teaching trends go in cycles, and she knows that if she devotes all her energies to this new scheme of work, she'll only see it replaced in a few years. She's also, frankly, sick of being encouraged to leave so that she can be replaced with a 'cheaper' new teacher. Is her experience not worth the money? Is her time spent at this school not valued or appreciated? Mona is beginning to feel like the answer to those questions is a resounding 'no'. So embrace the Monas, even though they refuse to dance at the school discos and tell you again that interactive whiteboards just 'weren't around in my day'. Be patient with them when they throw that new VR headset on the floor, filled with incandescent rage, and yes, stay calm even when they complain that this new initiative you spent months working on will only be 'too complicated'. Give them computer support, help them understand the new online assessment software, and for goodness' sake, be grateful that they hold up staff meetings with union-based questions because without the Monas of this world, nobody would be brave enough to say it, and we'd all be working for less.

I see you, Mona, and I thank you for your service.

Now to the dangers of comparison. The culture of some schools (not all, I hope) is changing. I've seen it become more competitive and business-like, to the point of turning colleagues against one another for better performance. For example, you may have had this conversation before:

'Have you heard? Mr Anderson got a "1" in his lesson observation?'
'Maybe you should try to be more like him - SLT love him!'

While, of course, there is much we can learn from one another, there comes a point when comparisons become dangerous. Particularly to those among us without a large amount of self-esteem. Certain academies can, shall we say, encourage friendly competition to motivate their staff, but this can quickly become toxic and demoralising. You can get to a place where you feel as though you're in the senior leadership team's 'bad books' or even worse, that they just don't like you. This leads to a decrease in productivity rather than an increase, as it can seem like there's 'no point in trying anyway'. Further, it can be damaging to judge yourself based on others. There are often 'star teachers' in a school. The kids love them, the parents love them - but that's just based on what they see from the outside and doesn't diminish your worth as a teacher. For more reserved, quieter members of staff especially, it can feel as though you aren't seen or appreciated, but your contributions are just as valuable, sometimes even more so than those who enjoy the limelight. Whether it's helping those more confident teachers set up their hair-brained talent shows behind the scenes or making sure that their class remains calm when they get a little over-excited, there is a space for you, and it's a vital one. So don't compare and despair - not all teachers are the same, but they are all worthy of praise and respect.

Back to a common problem in recent years - the desperation for ECTs (Early Career Teachers, formerly called NQTs (Newly Qualified Teachers)). Now, everyone started somewhere. It's a clichè but it's true. It's easy to resent new teachers as many academies choose to hire them over experienced staff. What have they got that you haven't? Well, they're cheaper. But to say that is the sole reason for their employment is to demean their worth. Of course, these decisions shouldn't be based on money, and I myself have been told that I'm 'too expensive' (how incredibly insulting) time and time again. However, within every new teacher is the potential of a brilliant and experienced one. There's a reason teacher retention is currently so low, and the ever-changing statistics of how many teachers leave the profession in their first three years are alarming. So while it's frustrating to lose out to these new, less experienced colleagues, try to remember that it isn't their fault. They didn't ask to be prioritised because they're willing to accept less. Often, they are hired for positions they are not yet ready for and end up leaving the profession in disgrace. It should be the employer's responsibility to hire someone appropriate for the role, and that's where your frustrations should lie. I have seen new teachers become truly incredible colleagues, but not without vital support from their peers. They want to learn from us; they want to be like us. Don't resent them, embrace them – you used to be them!

The mood hoover and the ingÈnue

Amelia, a bright-eyed and enthusiastic new teacher, bounded into the staff room with an energy that seemed almost unnatural for a Monday morning. Her radiant smile, like a beacon of optimism, clashed violently with the resigned faces of her more seasoned colleagues, who collectively sighed as she breezed in. The person least impressed by Amelia's infectious cheerfulness was none other than Barry, a self-proclaimed 'veteran' in the teaching profession. Barry had perfected the art of grumbling and had an uncanny ability to find the downside in every situation. His reputation as the resident 'Mood Hoover' preceded him, earning him the dubious honour of being a constant source of staffroom eye-rolls.

One day, during a particularly gloomy week where even the weather seemed to conspire against them, Amelia decided she had a mission – to convert Barry into a beacon of positivity. It was a challenge she undertook with the determination of a rookie superhero facing a formidable nemesis. Amelia began her campaign subtly, strategically placing motivational quotes around Barry's desk, hoping the power of positivity would seep into his subconscious. However, Barry's reaction was predictable – a dismissive scoff followed by an eye-roll that could rival any teenager's. Undeterred, Amelia shifted her approach. She decided to engage Barry in casual conversations, sneakily injecting optimism into the discourse. Every mention of a problem was met with a hopeful solution or a silver lining that seemed to elude Barry's ever-pessimistic perspective. One day, as Barry lamented the latest round of standardised testing and its impact on their teaching approach, Amelia chimed in with unwavering optimism.

'Barry, think about it – this is a chance for us to showcase the incredible progress our students have made! Look at the start of their books this year.'

Barry raised an eyebrow, sceptical but intrigued. It was a crack in his armour, and Amelia seized the opportunity.

'See,' Amelia pointed at a child's September writing before flicking forward to June, where they now were, 'look what you've done for her – that's you.' Barry scoffed but smiled softly. He had forgotten just how much that pupil had struggled when she came to him. Amelia began sharing success stories, highlighting moments of joy in the classroom, and subtly nudging Barry toward acknowledging the positives amidst the challenges.

As days turned into weeks, something miraculous happened. Barry's habitual scowl softened, and a glimmer of optimism emerged. Colleagues stared in disbelief as he joined in discussions about upcoming events with an unexpected eagerness. The tide was turning, and the transformation was a testament to the power of relentless optimism. Amelia, however, discovered an unexpected twist in this tale. While she had set out to change Barry, she found herself struggling in her own classroom. As the year drew to a close, Amelia lamented the hundreds of jobs she still had to do. One night, while desperately re-reading the National Curriculum, Amelia heard Barry enter her classroom.

'You okay, kid?' he inquired. 'It's very late.'

'Oh, you know,' Amelia replied, trying to maintain her characteristic optimism, 'just pootling along!'

Barry sat down next to her and cast an eye over her assessments. He pointed out the areas of the curriculum that overlapped, allowing her to assess multiple areas at once, saving her valuable time. He offered to read sections from her pupil's books while she scoured the assessment points. Over time, Amelia came to understand Barry's point of view and grew to appreciate his valuable insights and mentorship. Beneath the layers of gruff exterior, Barry possessed a wealth of experience and wisdom. As their interactions became more collaborative, it became evident that this unlikely duo was forging a connection that went beyond the surface.

In the end, the story of Amelia and Barry became a legend in the school – a tale of an optimistic newcomer who, against all odds, managed to bring a seasoned pessimist into the light. It underscored the notion that sometimes, the most unlikely pairings can lead to the most meaningful connections.

Lesson 6   Take a step back

Lesson objective: To gain some much-needed perspective of what's truly important.

Steps to success:

- Keep an open mind
- Don't sweat the small stuff

It was the second half of the Summer holidays and I had started having school dreams again. That morning I woke up having a panic attack. It was a particularly strange dream in which, of course, my classroom was totally different, and I was being given some kind of disciplinary for it being such a mess. (This may go some way to explain why my classroom is always tidy – what a weird fear to have, though.) Anyway, it was getting to that time again when I realised that my 'free time' was almost up. The countdown is real – we all feel it. It was about that time that I decided I needed some perspective. The 'countdown conundrum' is a common issue but a dangerous one. To count down to a 'time's up' scenario takes away our ability to feel free or happy once we return to work. Yes, we will be back to a structure that demands most of our time – but not all of it. Take this time to plan your back-to-school evenings. Dog walks, taking your kids to a nice play park, date nights, movie nights, and really whatever you want. Even if you just want some valuable alone time – make sure you have something in between the work-eat-sleep cycle that allows you to still be free.

After I started thinking about this, I took a philosophical moment to mentally 'zoom out'. This is where you need to keep an open mind as it gets a bit existential. Sometimes, when I allow myself these moments, I reflect upon the randomness of life. What is life? Why are we here? We are, at a very simplified level, a collection of atoms brought to life by happenstance and luck (unless you subscribe to an alternative theory, which is, of course, your right). Humanity has evolved to the point at which a piece of paper can end our world or a stern word from a superior can result in the most awful feelings of despair. To take a step back for a moment allows us to see how objectively ridiculous that is. I know that I personally care far too much about what others think of me, particularly at work. But to step back and see things differently takes a huge weight off my shoulders. Does it matter what one collection of atoms thinks about my collection of atoms? Honestly, no. Theoretically, I could pack up my family and move abroad at any time. I could win the lottery. I could die tomorrow. Life is random, so take a step back and don't let the small things become bigger than they have the right to be.

DOI: 10.4324/9781003506911-7

Of course, we have a duty of care to the children and young people we teach. At the base level, we have a moral and professional responsibility to keep them safe. Above that, I feel I must help them grow into 'good' people with 'good' life chances. Above that, however, I am going to try and stop worrying about whether they write 'h' the wrong way around. Obviously, I'm going to address it and correct it because that's what I'm technically being paid for. But if, despite my best efforts, Fahana still can't get her 'h' the right way around, it doesn't necessarily mean I'm a failure. It shouldn't make me lose sleep. If she's healthy, happy, and objectively 'better' than she was when she started the year, I need to be at peace with that.

I'll let you know if I manage this later on

Later in the year, once I had begun supply teaching, a similar moment occurred. In the staff-room of a school where I regularly worked, I had an interesting and yet predictable conversation with a colleague. The colleague in question was someone I had known for a while, and we got on well and often ate lunch together in the staff room. She was the reception teacher for that school, and we began talking about the recent changes our academies had made in our practice. She told me that her school's academy had recently forced her to formalise her teaching. Essentially, instead of learning through play, her reception and nursery mixed class now had structured writing, maths, and other lessons, where recording in books was non-negotiable. She explained how her previous phonics practice, which I genuinely saw as very good, was criticised by academy higher-ups. As she sent a child with cerebral palsy outside to use water and a paintbrush to mark make, she was asked why she didn't have more ambitions for this poor child whom she was leaving behind. Writing in water or sand was banned as it was deemed to be error-full and inaccurate, and so, one morning, I walked past the front entrance of the school to see a skip full of sand, water trays, and other perfectly good resources once deemed 'the best thing' and now deemed 'not good enough'. This poor woman, I thought, who has spent years honing her craft only to be told it's no longer the current trend. Imagine how horrified she was when I told her that my academy had also made changes but that these changes were the polar opposite. Our academy had encouraged us to abolish our structured writing lessons in favour of allowing the children to write in their play. While we still had maths lessons, the structure of the day was much less formal and much more focused on quality interactions with the children. Our multisensory approach to phonics, much like my colleague's, was praised by our academy, despite being criticised by hers. We had even been asked to introduce a 'rolling snack' which was, initially, a terrifying prospect. Rolling snack is how it sounds, a trolley full of deliciously tempting goodies, and a time window in which to take what you want. Yes, some children will be gaining a lot of weight this year in our setting, but we have to try these things to encourage independence and autonomy. Anyway, my point is not that one academy is right or wrong. My point is that, unfortunately, academies are very quick to jump on whatever research they have just read and enforce it quickly onto all of their schools. This is how two different schools at the same time can be given completely contradictory advice. This is where I feel it is easier to take a step back and gain some much-needed perspective. Because it is likely that in the next few years, you will be told to do the exact opposite all over again. So I told my colleague to hang in there and not take the criticisms personally. They were simply a knee-jerk reaction to an article she probably hadn't even read. I advised her not to spend hours worrying about how she was going to adjust to all of these new changes. The fads in teaching go round and round, and I have been teaching enough to see the circle complete at least once. I told her simply to retain as much of what she knew to be 'good practice', while still carrying out the things truly deemed 'non-negotiable'. I reminded her of the progress her children had made and pointed to the evidence that she is a good practitioner who knows what she's doing. At the end of the day, your intuition and experience cannot be bettered by those who have not been in a classroom recently. While you may have to play the game, that doesn't mean you have to lose yourself and your skill set in the process.

Perspective. It's a wonderful thing

I will now share with you a story about my good friend Mrs Hatton. Once a vibrant and passionate educator, Mrs Hatton found herself teetering on the edge of burn-out. Years of tirelessly devoting herself to her students had taken its toll, leaving her feeling drained and disillusioned. Each day became a relentless cycle of lesson planning, marking books, and attending meetings, leaving little time for self-care or reflection. One particularly gruelling week, Mrs Hatton felt herself reaching a breaking point. The weight of her responsibilities seemed impossible, and she questioned whether she had anything left to give. As she trudged through her daily routine, her enthusiasm waned, replaced by a sense of apathy and exhaustion.

One evening, as Mrs Hatton sat alone in her classroom, surrounded by stacks of books and half-finished lesson plans, she experienced a moment of clarity. The room, once a sanctuary of learning and creativity, now felt suffocating and oppressive. At that moment, she realised that she had lost sight of why she had become a teacher in the first place. Determined to regain her sense of purpose, Mrs Hatton decided to take a step back and reassess her priorities. She began by carving out time for self-care and making a conscious effort to engage in activities that brought her joy and relaxation. Whether it was taking leisurely walks in nature, indulging in her favourite hobbies, or simply enjoying a quiet cup of tea, she found solace in these moments of respite. With a renewed focus on her well-being, Mrs Hatton found that her perspective began to shift. She no longer felt overwhelmed by the demands of her job but rather approached each day with a sense of gratitude and enthusiasm. Instead of dwelling on the challenges, she chose to celebrate the small victories and moments of connection with her students.

With each passing day, Mrs Hatton felt a sense of purpose and fulfilment return to her life. She realised that by prioritising her own well-being, she was better equipped to support the needs of her students and foster a positive learning environment. It is at this point of our story you are probably folding your arms, and you would be right to do so. It wasn't long before Mrs Hatton's manager had called her into a meeting, having noticed that her previous high levels of perfectionism and completion had slipped. Mrs Hatton looked at the floor, disappointed in herself, but also angry. She explained – or she tried to – that what she was giving now was still perfectly adequate – better even – and that now, with an improved work-life balance, she was a better teacher for the children. This conversation made her manager pause, but not relent, as he informed her that he expected to see a return to her previous levels of excellence. After all, she managed it before.

   After several weeks of Mrs Hatton giving only 100% instead of her usual 120%, her manager called her in for another meeting.

'I think you know what I'm going to say, Julie,' he began. Julie looked at the floor again, but somehow found it within herself to ask a question.

'Are the children not making progress?' Her manager stammered momentarily. This increased her confidence. 'Are they suffering? Have I neglected their needs or their learning?' The manager went to reply, but Julie was gaining confidence now. 'Have I failed to teach any objectives of the National Curriculum? Have I missed any after-school meetings or extracurricular events? Has my classroom become an unsafe environment?'

'Well, actually,' he interrupted, clearly slightly annoyed. 'Your borders are coming away from the wall on your maths display.' Mrs Hatton looked dumbstruck. 'And Mr Ackton noticed that you've stopped working in your classroom at lunchtime. I also saw you leave at 4 pm last Wednesday when usually you would stay until six. We're just concerned that something may be wrong?' Julia paused, drawing on all of her inner strength.

'Other than the borders, has any aspect of my performance slipped?' Her manager paused.

'Well, we haven't seen anything yet but –'

'Is it mandatory to work through lunch?'

'No, but –'

'If I complete my work by 4 pm, am I permitted then to leave, especially considering that I arrive at school at 7 am each morning?' Her manager sighed, defeated but not yet admitting defeat. Julie knew that these were all perfectly valid points but that, within the realms of education, working late and eating lunch at your desk was very much expected of you. She was still determined to fight, however. She was dismissed from the office with mumblings of work ethic and professionalism burning in her ears.

I would love to tell you that this story ends with her manager becoming more reasonable or understanding of the sacrifices Mrs Hatton had made and why she had made them. Sadly, however, it was up to Mrs Hatton to change. Only when she was able to let go of the guilt her manager tried to force upon her – easier to do once she began to keep a track record of her and her class' successes – was she able to happily maintain this newfound work-life balance. It took a change of perspective for Mrs Hatton to find peace in a career that continued to demand so much from her.

Lesson 7   Work smarter, not harder

Lesson objective: To adopt strategies to better manage our time and increase efficiency.

Steps to success:

- Look for the most efficient ways to complete your tasks – especially admin
- Lower those standards of perfectionism!

A buzz phrase at the moment, 'work smarter, not harder' is the new favourite saying of our deputy head. He makes a good point, though. Why waste hours reinventing the wheel? Now, I'm not suggesting that we all get those new AI websites to write our reports for us (although some teachers have *definitely* suggested that to me!), but there are ways of making your life easier without cutting corners. Take that new planning format, for instance. You could spend hours re-typing your perfectly good existing plans into it from scratch or you could (and I know this won't be a revelation for us all) 'copy and paste' from your old plan. Copy and paste is your friend – and a pro tip, highlight the text you want, hold down Ctrl+C to copy and Ctrl+V to paste it into your new document. Again, I know this will be obvious to some of you, but I am catering to the less technically minded amongst us, and please don't feel ashamed. We all have our strengths. I am also fairly certain that in the coming years, AI will become a useful tool in this instance – if there isn't already some kind of AI software that transfers information from one format to another, there really should be.

   Paperwork is, unfortunately, going to be the thing that takes up most of your precious time. For example, a few years ago, I had a particularly high number of children with special educational needs in my class (11 out of 30), and so I had a *mountain* of paperwork to update each half-term. I had target sheets, behaviour plans, 'One-page profiles' that were, in fact, three pages long and so on, and so on. To save my time and sanity, I would have these handy as we went through the term to scribble notes on as we went along. That way, when it came to the inevitable deadline, I just needed to write up my existing notes rather than coming up with everything from scratch. It doesn't eliminate a job, but it does break it down into smaller bite-sized pieces. As well as a statistically challenging class, the expectations for the year were very high. I was told in no uncertain terms that a 'maximum of two' children per class 'but ideally one' were allowed to 'not make GLD (good level of development)' this year. In layman's terms, I had to get 28 children over an increasingly challenging finish line. For my own sanity, I assessed them early on. Not with tests or nonsense like that – they were 4, don't be silly. I spent time

DOI: 10.4324/9781003506911-8

with them, playing games and doing activities. After ten years, it's fairly easy to get a sense of those who are developmentally ready for school and those who may need a boost. Anyway, to cut a long story short, I had five. Not five children who might not make it, but five children who definitely *would*. You see, the COVID pandemic hit child development *hard*. We were finding that the majority of our classes just hadn't developed the necessary personal, social, and emotional skills they needed to even begin to contemplate something as complex as maths or writing. Furthermore, the number of special school places for children with complex needs was vastly lacking, and so we had several children who, in any other year, would not have even *been* in our setting because, frankly, their level of need made it unsafe for them and those around them. So there I was 5 children down, 23 to go, and changing nappies for the first time in my career. As the terms passed, the pressure slowly dropped as others realised the challenges we were facing with this cohort. By Christmas, I had 10 children who were now at the 'correct' developmental level and by spring, 15. While these numbers alone (that's only 50%) may seem poor, because I put the time in to assess them initially, I could focus on the *progress*. That was my saving grace. It didn't change the expectations, but it changed the narrative and my mental well-being. Work smarter, not harder – show them the data that celebrates your achievements. It will be there.

Now this next section, as I begin to write it, is largely uncharted territory. However, I would wager that by the time this book greets you, many more advances will have been made. I am talking, of course, about AI. The free AI model I currently use to assist me in promoting my first book has helped me enormously. Where I struggle to blow my own horn, the AI will do it for me, elegantly and intuitively. While I haven't yet delved into this for my teaching, the implications are huge. Take this simple prompt for example, and see what comes out in a matter of seconds:

> 'Plan a forty-five-minute lesson for Year 1 children based on the British National Curriculum with the learning objective of adding two numbers together (under twenty).' The output below was produced using Chat GPT.

The result, as you can see, is nothing short of mind-blowing – for me at least!

Chat GPT Software response:

'Sure, I'd be happy to help you plan a lesson on adding two numbers together for Year 1 children based on the British National Curriculum. Here's a lesson plan that you can follow:'

Title: Adding Two Numbers Together (Under Twenty)

Objective: By the end of the lesson, the Year 1 children will be able to add two numbers together under twenty.

Materials Needed:

Whiteboard and marker
Number flashcards (0-20)
Counters or small objects (e.g. buttons, beans, etc.)
Worksheets for practice (optional)

Introduction (5 minutes)

Begin by introducing the topic of adding two numbers together. Ask the children if they know what addition means and what it is used for.

Show them the number flashcards and ask them to identify the numbers. Then, choose two numbers under twenty and ask the children to add them together using the flashcards. Write the sum on the whiteboard.

Repeat with a few more pairs of numbers, encouraging the children to join in and help you write the answers on the board.

Main Activity (25 minutes)

Divide the children into pairs and give each pair some counters or small objects. Explain that they will be adding two numbers together using the counters.

Give each pair a number card with a number under twenty on it. Ask them to put that many counters on the table.

Then, give them another number card and ask them to put that many counters on the table next to the first set of counters.

Ask the children to count the total number of counters they have and tell you the answer. Write the sum on the whiteboard.

Repeat with a few more pairs of numbers, encouraging the children to swap partners so that they get to work with different numbers.

Assessment (10 minutes)

Give the children some worksheets to complete. These worksheets should have a series of addition problems with two numbers under twenty, and spaces for the children to write the answers.

Walk around the classroom and observe the children as they work on the worksheets, offering guidance and support as needed.

Conclusion (5 minutes)

Ask the children to share what they learned today about adding two numbers together. Ask them to give some examples of problems they can now solve, and encourage them to practice their new skill at home.

Thank the children for their hard work and participation in the lesson.

That's it! This lesson plan should take approximately 45 minutes and help Year 1 children learn how to add two numbers together under twenty.

(End of message)

I look back on the gruelling year of my life spent studying for my PGCE (postgraduate certificate in education) and sigh. How many hours would this have saved me? Of course, I would advise you to at least edit this lesson plan to tailor it to your particular class. Additionally, there is the ethical argument - by buying into these new systems, are we making ourselves obsolete? Perhaps. But in my premise of 'work smarter, not harder', this has to be an option you consider in a tight pinch.

Another practical strategy to consider is the use of technology to streamline administrative tasks. For instance, instead of manually marking piles of books, explore digital tools like online quizzes or automated assessment systems. These tools not only save time but also provide instant feedback to pupils, allowing for more efficient assessment and intervention. Furthermore, leverage the power of collaborative platforms to enhance productivity. Rather than reinventing the wheel with lesson planning, join forces with fellow educators to share resources and ideas. Websites like TES Resources or collaborative platforms such as Google Drive offer a treasure trove of lesson plans, worksheets, and teaching materials created by teachers for teachers. By tapping into this collective knowledge pool, you can access high-quality resources with minimal effort. Another area where you can work smarter is in classroom management. Implementing behaviour management software such as Track-it Lights or Class Dojo can prevent disruptive behaviour before it occurs. These visual interfaces constantly remind children what they are working towards and the expectations for behaviour. This can save you time trying to find stickers, and they can even interact with them themselves – awarding themselves points when allowed, cutting down on more time-draining tasks for you.

In conclusion, working smarter, not harder, is about adopting strategic approaches to teaching that maximise efficiency and effectiveness. By embracing technology, collaborating with colleagues, implementing proactive classroom management techniques, and prioritising what's important, you can create a more sustainable and fulfilling teaching experience. So take a step back, assess your current practices, and explore innovative ways to optimise your workflow. Your students – and your sanity – will thank you for it.

Hey you! Yes, you, the staff member reluctantly skimming through this latest 'required reading'. Has the Senior Leadership Team gone yet? No? Don't worry, they'll get bored soon. Or they'll have a 'very important meeting' to get to. Make a cuppa and keep going. I'll be back.

Lesson 8   Don't even think about Ofsted

Lesson objective: Don't even get me started ...

Steps to success:

- Ugh
- The system is broken
- Don't let it break you

One Monday afternoon, in bed recovering from COVID, I got a call from my assistant head to say that Ofsted would finally be coming in tomorrow, and it would be better if I could be there. I was actually relieved. In a few short days, it would finally be over. The months and months of waiting for them, preparing for them, agonising over their ill-informed judgements of the blood, sweat. and tears we poured into every day of our working lives and it would be for (hopefully) a few years. Our head tentatively spoke of 'getting our love for the job back' after this 'one last push'. Don't get me wrong, it was possibly the hardest two days of my life, and we were extremely poorly treated, in my view. There were mind games played and criticisms made that didn't take into account any real-world context or completely reasonable mitigations. However, now, writing this, it is over.

You can prepare and you can plan, but who is it for? I've worked in schools where everything we did was for Ofsted. I've worked in schools where it was geared more towards the children, and trust me, the latter is more effective. I've heard it said that you can only be judged as 'Outstanding' if you tick their boxes and use their buzzwords. If that's the case, you can keep your 'Outstanding' because that's not why I do this job, and it shouldn't be a qualifier for judging a school. We are here for the children, not for Ofsted. We do what we do to improve the life chances of children, not to tick a box. So don't tell me that my numbers on a spreadsheet don't match your otherworldly expectations and then ignore me when I tell you, eyes bursting with pride, that a little boy with an anger problem hasn't hurt anyone in two weeks. When I tell you that the reason that little girl hasn't made progress this term is because her home life has been dangerously unstable, how dare you roll your eyes when I say at least we've kept her safe and happy. That is enough. That should be enough.

I told you not to get me started, and this is exactly why.

Without wishing to be sued or fired or mysteriously disappear in the night, I will wrap it up here. What you need to know, though, is that yes, Ofsted is going to be there, at least for now, whether we agree with them or not. However, you're not there for them, and no one should

DOI: 10.4324/9781003506911-9

be telling you otherwise. Remember who you're there for, do your very best for them, and the rest should be more than good enough for whoever might be judging you that day. So for the rest of the chapter, I will try my best to remain objective and analytical.

Objective analysis: unravelling the impact of Ofsted on the educational landscape

The Office for Standards in Education, Children's Services and Skills, commonly known as Ofsted, has long been a central figure in the educational landscape of the United Kingdom. Established to ensure high standards in schools and other educational institutions, Ofsted has undeniably played a crucial role in shaping policies and practices. However, the impact of Ofsted on the education sector is a topic that has stirred considerable debate. This analysis explores the negative repercussions of Ofsted on educators, students, and the overall educational environment, supported by research and references.

1. The culture of compliance

One of the overarching criticisms of Ofsted is the creation of a culture of compliance within educational institutions. The stringent inspection processes and the consequential grading system often lead schools to prioritise meeting the criteria set by Ofsted over genuine educational innovation and improvement. Research by Ball (2003) highlights how schools, driven by the fear of inspection outcomes, tend to adopt a 'teaching to the test' approach, narrowing the curriculum and stifling creativity.

The pressure to conform to Ofsted's expectations can result in a one-size-fits-all approach, neglecting the diverse needs of students and inhibiting the development of critical thinking skills. The focus on measurable outcomes, while important to assess performance, often overshadows the broader goals of education, such as fostering a love for learning and nurturing well-rounded individuals.

2. Stress and well-being of educators

Ofsted inspections are inherently stressful events for educators. The anticipation of inspection, the intense scrutiny during the process, and the potential ramifications of unfavourable outcomes contribute to elevated stress levels among teachers and school leaders. A study by Johnson et al. (2005) found a significant correlation between Ofsted inspections and increased stress and anxiety levels among educators.

The fear of negative inspection outcomes can lead to burn-out, reduced job satisfaction, and in some cases, a higher attrition rate within the teaching profession. The focus on accountability and the consequences tied to inspection results place an immense burden on educators, diverting their attention from pedagogical innovation and student engagement to a more defensive, compliance-driven mindset.

3. Impact on student well-being

While Ofsted's primary goal is to ensure the quality of education, the pressure it exerts on schools can inadvertently affect the well-being of students. The emphasis on exam results and performance metrics may lead to a narrow, exam-focused curriculum that neglects the holistic development of students. Research by Gewirtz et al. (1995) suggests that the account-ability measures associated with Ofsted inspections contribute to a performative culture that prioritises quantitative outcomes over the well-being of students.

Furthermore, the anxiety experienced by educators during the inspection process may inadvertently transfer to students, creating an atmosphere of stress and pressure within schools. The focus on achieving high grades and meeting Ofsted expectations may over-shadow the nurturing of a positive and supportive learning environment.

4. Impact on creativity and innovation

Ofsted's influence on education has been criticised for stifling creativity and innovation in teaching practices. The pressure to conform to established norms and criteria can discourage educators from adopting unconventional or experimental teaching methods. Research by Robinson (2011) emphasises the importance of fostering creativity in education, stating that standardised assessments and stringent inspections can hinder the development of creative thinking skills in students.

The emphasis on meeting Ofsted's expectations may dissuade educators from exploring alternative approaches that could better cater to the diverse learning needs of students. The fear of negative inspection outcomes may create a risk-averse culture within schools, where educators are hesitant to deviate from established practices, even if those practices may not be the most effective for certain students.

5. Widening socio-economic disparities

Ofsted's focus on performance metrics and examination results has been criticised for con-tributing to widening socio-economic disparities in education. Research by Reay et al. (2001) suggests that schools in economically disadvantaged areas may face additional challenges in meeting Ofsted's criteria, potentially leading to negative inspection outcomes. The conse-quences of poor inspection results can perpetuate a cycle of underperformance and limited resources for schools in disadvantaged communities. I can confirm that the Ofsted inspection I was subjected to at a school in a deprived area presented significantly more challenges, specifically around attendance and pupils with English as an additional language.

Furthermore, the pressure to improve inspection outcomes may lead schools to priori-tise interventions for borderline students, potentially neglecting the needs of those who are already excelling or struggling significantly. This focus on the 'middle ground' to meet inspec-tion criteria can inadvertently exacerbate existing educational inequalities. Unfortunately, I have seen this happen – with some children being 'written off' by some as they were unlikely to meet the end-of-year goals, even with significant support.

6. Inconsistencies in inspection outcomes

Critics of Ofsted point to the inconsistencies in inspection outcomes, raising questions about the reliability and validity of the inspection process. Research by Brown et al. (2016) highlights variations in inspection judgments, with similar schools receiving different ratings based on the inspection team and the timing of the visit. Such inconsistencies not only undermine the credibility of Ofsted but also create a sense of unfairness among educators.

Inaccurate or inconsistent inspection outcomes can have serious consequences for schools, affecting their reputation, recruitment efforts, and overall standing in the educational community. The lack of standardisation in inspection procedures and outcomes diminishes the trust educators and the public place in the reliability of Ofsted assessments.

Conclusion

While Ofsted was established with the noble intention of ensuring high standards in education, its impact on the educational sector has been far-reaching and, in many cases, detrimental. From fostering a culture of compliance to negatively affecting the well-being of educators and students, the criticisms against Ofsted are supported by research and academic perspectives. The educational landscape calls for a comprehensive evaluation of the inspection system, aiming for a balance between accountability and the promotion of a diverse, innovative, and student-centric learning environment.

***

Later addendum

Interestingly, since I began writing this book, Ofsted has hit headlines for exactly these reasons. Particularly regarding mental health, Ofsted has come under fire for damaging the profession and, specifically, the people in it. Recent headlines have brought to light a concerning trend within the educational landscape – the increasing number of headteacher suicides. In response to this crisis, the Office for Standards in Education, Children's Services and Skills (Ofsted) has taken a notable step by introducing mandatory mental health training for its inspectors. This chapter delves into the news surrounding Ofsted's initiative, analysing the challenges faced by headteachers, the implications of this mandatory training, and the broader context of mental health in the education sector. But will it change the way schools and teachers feel about 'The Big O'?

The role of a headteacher is undeniably challenging, with responsibilities ranging from academic leadership to managing staff, budgets, and the overall well-being of the school community. In recent years, a disturbing trend has emerged – an increasing number of headteachers succumbing to the pressures of their roles and taking their own lives. The reasons behind these tragedies are complex and multifaceted, often involving a combination of professional stress, unrealistic expectations, and personal challenges. Research by the National Association of Head Teachers (NAHT) reveals alarming statistics, indicating a rise in stress-related illnesses among school leaders. The relentless demands of the job, coupled with external pressures such as stringent inspections, have created a high-stakes environment for headteachers. The mental health toll is evident, prompting urgent interventions to address the well-being of educational leaders.

In response to the concerning rise in headteacher suicides, Ofsted has acknowledged the need for a proactive approach to mental health within the education sector. The regulatory body has introduced mandatory mental health training for its inspectors, recognising the pivotal role they play in shaping the experiences of school leaders during inspections. The training aims to equip inspectors with the skills and awareness necessary to recognise signs of mental health struggles among school staff, particularly headteachers.

Ofsted's decision to implement mandatory mental health training for its inspectors carries significant implications for the education sector. These implications extend beyond the immediate context of inspections and contribute to a broader conversation about prioritising mental health in educational leadership. With mental health training, Ofsted inspectors are likely to approach their evaluations with increased sensitivity to the well-being of school leaders. This may manifest in a more nuanced understanding of the challenges faced by headteachers, acknowledging the human aspect of their roles. By integrating mental health considerations into the inspection framework, Ofsted is signalling a shift in perspective. Well-being is increasingly being recognised as a critical component of school leadership, and this awareness may prompt schools to prioritise the mental health of their staff. The question is – will it be a catalyst for a shift in how educators are treated and expected to work? I certainly hope so.

Sources for this chapter

Ball, S. J. (2003). The teacher's soul and the terrors of performativity. *Journal of Education Policy*, 18(2), 215-228.

Brown, C., Durbin, B., Evans, K., & Carr, M. (2016). Ofsted's role in shaping policy on school improvement: Rhetoric and reality. *Journal of Education Policy*, 31(3), 294-311.

Gewirtz, S., Ball, S. J., & Bowe, R. (1995). *Markets, Choice, and Equity in Education*. Open University Press.

Johnson, S., Cooper, C., Cartwright, S., Donald, I., Taylor, P., & Millet, C. (2005). The experience of work-related stress across occupations. *Journal of Managerial Psychology*, 20(2), 178-187.

Reay, D., David, M., & Ball, S. J. (2001). Making a difference?: Institutional habituses and higher education choice. *Sociological Research Online*, 5(4), 1-17.

Robinson, K. (2011). *Out of Our Minds: Learning to be Creative*. Capstone.

Has your assistant head left the room yet? Oh, they're still fiddling with the sound on the smart board. Got it. Don't worry, they'll leave soon.

Lesson 9   What about supply teaching?

Lesson objective: Consider your options – there are many kinds of teaching roles out there.

Steps to success:

- With less pressure comes less responsibility
- Look at your finances
- Think about what you want from your career

After having my first novel published, I decided to take the terrifying financial leap towards part-time teaching. At the time, after a huge amount of budgeting and stress, it was a financially safe move. However, what I didn't know was that my life would shortly thereafter be turned upside down, making it slightly riskier than I had first anticipated. Anyway, that's another story, which I will possibly write in the years to come.

Anyway, part-time teaching is, as I discovered, very different to full-time teaching. There are definite pros and cons, and I imagine it varies widely from school to school, so bear in mind that my opinion is based on one school and one school alone. That being said, going part-time at my school has been bliss. Thankfully, my job-share partner is a literal angel, she's organised, we communicate well, she's understanding, and we both have the same mindset when it comes to teaching and children. She makes it incredibly easy. Having the job I previously had but with the responsibility and time itself cut in half made it feel as though I could breathe again. Unfortunately, the money halved too. However, even my mother, the most financially rigorous person I knew, told me that sometimes there are things more important than money and that my happiness was one of those things. I am, at the time of writing, delighted to be part-time. I still have a class of my own that I love and follow throughout the year so that I can watch them grow, while also having more time to myself. I had always wondered about part-time teachers, as there is a sort of snobbery around them in some places, viewing them as 'less ideal' for a child than one full-time teacher. There is a perceived lack of consistency, and sometimes the part-time teacher with fewer hours is seen more as a supply teacher. However, coming in on a Thursday with bright eyes and a metaphorically bushy tail, I have seen the advantages that having two part-time teachers can have. Our brilliant class is lucky to have twice the creativity, twice the ideas, and twice the people that they know they feel safe and loved with. I honestly don't see a downside. If your job share teacher was reluctant to communicate or employed a very different teaching style to you, then I can see

DOI: 10.4324/9781003506911-10

that this may be a nightmare situation. Luckily, that has been the opposite of my experience. So from this, I can conclude that part-time is infinitely better than full-time for one's mental health – but that's not exactly a surprise now, is it? I'm sure if we could all afford to be part-time teachers, we would.

Now, revisiting my slight midlife crisis and financial peril for a moment. Due to some significant upheaval in my personal life, I had to take supply work to cover my three 'free' days, which I had hoped to allocate to time spent writing. Ah well, life often gets in the way of our dreams, doesn't it? This meant that essentially, I was still a full-time teacher, just in many different places. I don't necessarily recommend this, as I do feel pulled between many worlds, and it can be stressful doing both. I have considered full-time supply, but it comes down to finances, as the pay is significantly less than the higher points of the teachers' pay scale. Supply can also vary wildly, as I will explain below.

I know many happy teachers who are full-time supply teachers and love it. The greatest assets of this career choice include flexibility, decreased responsibility and pressure, and generally far less workload. The flip side of that, however, is that you don't have a guaranteed income – no good for someone with a mortgage to pay like me. Additionally, you don't get to know one class and one group of children particularly well, unless you are given a recurring or longer-term role, which does happen. I met a lovely supply teacher in my last school who tends to take half-term or even term-length placements. These are cropping up more and more as teachers leave mid-year (usually newer teachers who didn't quite know what they were getting themselves in for), and she does a great job – swooping in to take care of them until their next teacher is appointed. Getting to know a class is not important to all teachers, but it is something that I love and value about teaching. Making that bond and making those relationships with those children is really important to me, and it helps enormously with behaviour management. Going in as a supply teacher, it doesn't matter if you have the best behaviour management strategy in the world, the number one thing for good behaviour management is making those relationships, and as a supply teacher, you just don't get the chance to do that. A few other issues one encounters while supply teaching is the dreaded 'FOMO – Fear Of Missing Out'. In a permanent position in a school, you get to do all of the 'fun stuff' like trips and World Book Days, but as a supply teacher, you miss all of that, which can feel disheartening. It's also easy to lose track if you are all over the place all of the time, and you can start to feel out of control. Luckily for me, I have been fortunate enough to be asked back to one school repeatedly, allowing me to build a relationship with those children, which I loved. It was a lovely little village school, and I would go back there in a heartbeat. Other schools I have been to have been … more challenging. This is to be expected, of course, and once you've done the day there, if you hate it, you never have to go back. However, that day can seem like the longest day of your life.

For example, earlier this month I was in a school in a deprived area as a supply teacher. I had a quick toilet break, and on the wall, I observed a motivational poster reading 'It's ok to cry. Clouds do it all the time.' How depressingly evocative of the teaching profession, I thought to myself. If you, in your place of work, need a sign reminding you that it's okay to cry, what are you doing? What is this country doing to its teachers? Because it didn't make me sad, it made me laugh. Because teachers crying in toilets is now just a running joke. We all do it, we all joke about doing it, and we are all so used to it that it just becomes a way of teaching life. But imagine if every job found it acceptable for their employees to cry in the storerooms or the toilets regularly. Would the working conditions of that job not then be called into question? As I worked through this particular day of supply teaching, I heard more and more conversations from staff about their struggles in the workplace. I left work that day feeling deflated and scrolling, as teachers often do, on job sites for 'inspiration'.

Later that week I was sent, just for the afternoon, to a small local school. I felt confident that this would be an easy few hours. I was misinformed. I entered the classroom to be pelted with banana skin by a child who, I quickly assessed, was likely neurodivergent and clearly overstimulated by a mainstream classroom. At least I knew it wasn't personal, as he hadn't even learned my name by the time the banana made contact with my face. It quickly became apparent, however, as the afternoon continued, with several highly dysregulated characters and no teaching assistant in sight, that this would be one of the longer afternoons of my life.

But it's not all doom and gloom, of course, let me tell you about one of the best supply teaching days I have had. It was the Monday after half term, and there was no way I was going to accept a supply job that day. I had spent the half term staying with my brother in London and attending many of his exciting theatre events. It was brilliant but exhausting. So when I woke up to a message at 7:45 am after just seven hours of sleep (I'm very cranky with less than eight), I was surprised to find myself considering saying yes. Granted, my main motivation was financial, as I had spent a fair amount whilst in London, but I was also surprisingly optimistic about a day spent with children.

Upon arrival, nobody quite knew where I was supposed to be or who I was covering – always a good sign! I waited in the staff room and began to witness some very strange behaviour … The receptionist just walked past me singing. The teaching assistants are … smiling? The teachers seem awake, and not devastated by this. What is their secret? I must discover this, I thought to myself. Looking in the cupboard for mugs, I discovered one with the school emblem and the phrase 'Lockdown Learning Hero' emblazoned on the side. I assumed that these were gifts to the staff during a difficult time. I liked this. Most schools tend to just do the obligatory tub of celebrations, or worse, stock the toilets with sanitary towels and call it a 'well-being basket', but this seemed more purposeful and thoughtful. Also, instead of the empty motivational phrases adorning the staffroom walls, they had pertinent information from a local mental health support team with a link to a staff survey. They were actively encouraging staff to be honest about how they were feeling at work and to feed it back to an external source. This is unheard of. There are posters in the staff room, but they haven't got anything to do with how sad people might be feeling or how appreciated people might be feeling if they only looked at this tokenistic poster. The posters here, however … they were just nice posters. Pleasing to look at, aesthetically complimenting colours and shapes. I think there may have been from a French food festival, based on the loopy writing I could translate.

Eventually, my rightful place was located (a simple miscommunication between the office and SLT), and I was taken up some stairs to the two classes situated in the converted attic of the building. This quiet little niche suited me quite well, and I happily walked into a chattering of Year 4 students, midway through their morning learning. Normally, of course, I would have arrived before them – but the lateness of the call meant that I was slightly delayed. It was shortly after this that I discovered a second potential reason for the staff's happiness. The planning was … ostensibly, no more than a couple of sentences. I had a series of hyperlinks on a slide show and the 'Learning Objective: To understand how adverts use language to persuade'. The hyperlinks, predictably, were links to four short video advertisements for theme parks (one from the eighties with Terry Wogan – what a throwback!), but how this was meant to fill an hour, I had no idea.

Enter the dragon. The dragon in question being Puffles, my loyal plush assistant. After analysing the clips in question for persuasive phrases and convincing conversation, Puffles decided to give the class a challenge. Could they convince him to buy something mundane or ordinary using persuasive language? He gave an example by picking up a glue stick and enthusiastically extolling the strength of its stickiness and the shininess of its label – obviously exaggerating to give them an idea of where to go. Nervous at first, a couple of children volunteered to sell Puffles 'the best biro in the world' or 'the ruler – don't draw a line without it!' As more children succeeded, with Puffles excitedly racking up a collection of surplus stationery, the rest of the class became excited and eager to join in too. By the end of the lesson, they had all mastered the art of persuasion and had, I believe, achieved the objective as well as having fun. I thought to myself, 'Well done, you smashed that!' It's not often we as teachers get to have moments like that – especially in our own, permanent classes where things are generally pre-planned and predictable. So something I enjoy about supply teaching is the thing I initially lived in fear of – the freedom! If there's no planning – don't panic – you trained for this! You finally have the chance to be creative, and if it doesn't work – who cares? You don't have to go back there again. As long as you try, that's all you can do, and sometimes, on those wonderful days, you'll smash it.

So with two contrasting stories, I can confirm that no two days of supply teaching are ever the same (much the same as with any teaching, really). But if you're in the financial position to give it a try and you aren't sure about throwing the towel in on teaching entirely – then it's certainly an avenue worth exploring.

The next chapter is going to be a difficult one, but I can see SLT making their excuses to run to 'photocopy something', so they'll be out of your hair soon, and we'll be able to really talk.

Lesson 10   The silent expectations

Lesson objective: Don't get snowed under by the 'silent expectations'.

Steps to success:

- Check your contract
- Remember you're only human

Towards the end of a particularly difficult term, a friend recommended an online group to me entitled 'Life after teaching: Exit the classroom and thrive.' As the name suggests, this was a group for teachers looking to find an alternative career that would utilise their existing skills. Members of the group who had found success outside of teaching frequently advised those desperately trying to move on. One of the harder things about teaching is that you can feel trapped within it – any other career with the same qualifications (provided you don't have any bonus skills up your sleeve) usually comes with a pay cut and a large one at that. Therefore it's easy to feel stuck and resentful, as many teachers don't feel like they have a way out. Anyway, at first, the group seemed like a safe space, full of support and camaraderie. However, as the messages began to pile up, they only fuelled my depression surrounding the more difficult aspects of teaching. While there is relief in a shared perspective, particularly when others have it worse than you, the following messages (posted anonymously) didn't exactly fill me with hope for the profession. One post read:

I am a teacher
I am an outstanding teacher, who cares for the lives of young people.
I am an incredible teacher, who plans effectively to meet the needs of every learner.
I am a wonderful teacher, who makes learning fun, engaging and interesting.
I am a passionate teacher, who creates a positive space for children to feel safe.
I am a driven teacher, who unpicks data and supports learners to catch up.
I am a super teacher, who provides quality feedback and celebrates great progress.

I am a teacher, who wants to leave the classroom.
I am a person who wants to feel valued.
I am an individual who wants to be respected for their knowledge and expertise.

DOI: 10.4324/9781003506911-11

I am sad, stressed, never good enough, never thanked or appreciated, never lifted up or
  praised teacher. I am a person hurt by a broken system of fear and manipulation. I am anx-
  ious. I am unsure of who I can trust.

I am replaceable.
I am beaten down.
I am … no longer … a teacher.

- Anonymous

This post gained hundreds of empathetic 'likes' from hundreds of teachers feeling exactly the
same way. This is the problem with our profession, and it has nothing to do with the children,
it's the silent expectations.

   'Hi all, we have a great deal of staff absence at the moment, so I don't feel as though I can
take any time off work. However, my father is dying (he will pass within the next two or three
days) and driving the two hours to see him after work every day is really taking its toll. Would
I be punished for asking for time off?'

   The answer in any other career would be obvious – bereavement and family crisis are usually perfectly acceptable reasons for a leave of absence – but the answers provided by fellow
teachers were less than encouraging. One member wrote:

> It depends on how well you cope with the guilt! I took two weeks off last year when my
> mother passed and I was made to feel so guilty about it. I was then denied permission to
> go to her funeral as I had already had so much time off and we were short-staffed.

Another member wrote:

> I was told earlier this year that I had been to 'too many funerals' this year and that I
> would have to be more selective. About the close friends and family around me that
> died? Okay then …

Thankfully, the majority of messages urged the original poster to take the time, although
there may be consequences, as ultimately, this would be their last time with their father. The
exchanges, however, just reminded me of the 'silent expectations' of teaching.

Silent expectation #1: never take time off

There is an enormous sense of pride bestowed on those teachers who are 'never off sick'
and certainly more respect is given to those who come into work despite sickness. Staff with
chronic health issues are often labelled as 'always off' or 'unreliable', and those with children
are seen as a liability as they may need to take additional time off to take care of them.

   While there are procedures and policies for taking time off, the number of sick days you
are entitled to before a 'trigger point' is reached is often extremely low. One year I caught
a stomach bug from a school trip (the coach journey home was utterly disgusting), which
developed into a form of norovirus. The following month, I was knocked over by a child and
slipped my disc. These two periods of absence triggered an 'absence meeting' as they were
'too close together'. The umbrage I took with this, despite being an established policy, was no
doubt influenced by the fact that both of these ailments were sustained while working and

would not have occurred had I not been working. The result of this was that I was too afraid to take any time off for the next calendar year as this would trigger the next point of the absence scale. This meant I ended up coming into work when my disc slipped again, propped up by cushions and codeine. This is why it is so normal to see teachers going to work unwell – the fear of being absent just makes the time off more stressful than the pain of going in. And this is without the expectations placed on you to prepare and resource the cover teacher should you be away.

Silent expectation #2: unpaid overtime

Did you know that a teacher's paid, contracted hours per day are only six – 8 am–12 pm and 1 pm–3 pm generally. In reality, no teacher works these hours. I usually arrive at school around quarter to eight, and leave between four and five, on a good day. Some days I am there until 6 pm. This doesn't take into account thrice-yearly parents' evenings or school trips which often run late. The other day I took the school choir to London and was working from 8 am to 2 am the following day. This was not even a working day for me, since I had begun my part-time contract at this point, but I was told I would still not be paid for this. I managed to, with some reluctance, secure a day in lieu, which I was happy with at least. Next Monday (another non-working day) I am coming in for a meeting, which is seen as voluntary. Then you have the 'events' you are expected to give up your time to assist with, such as school discos, summer fayres and Christmas performances.

There is a line or two in every teacher's contract that is used to justify this phenomenon, and it usually reads something like this:

> In addition to the hours for which you can be directed, a teacher may work such reasonable additional hours as necessary. This can include time for planning and preparing lessons and assessing pupils' work. However, the number of additional hours cannot be specified by your school. As a consequence, it does not count towards your hours of directed time. All work undertaken during non-directed time is determined by the individual teacher and it is up to you to exercise your professional judgement in how you manage this.

Up to your professional judgment? Ah, so if we don't get our planning done because our child has a birthday, and we make the 'professional judgement' to let it slide – would that be acceptable? Unlikely. If we have worked every evening this week and just need Friday night to wind down before the childcare demands of the weekend but that data is due Monday morning – is it really up to our professional judgement?

Silent expectation #3: if you're unhappy, you hate children

This is a difficult one for me. For the first eight to nine years of my career, I was THAT teacher. You know the type – always at the summer fayres, happy to perform at 'Teacher's Got Talent' and generally always ready to 'get stuck in' for the children because it was fun. I relished being that teacher. And yes, at times I looked down on those who never got involved with the extra stuff, but for the past two years, I have struggled. For many reasons, most of which are confined to my personal life, I have lost my 'fun' in teaching. For my mental health, I have stepped back from school discos and not volunteered for as many fayres and events. I want to, but I just don't have the strength. I feel as though it has been beaten out of me, and all I have strength left for is the children. Looking in from the outside, it may seem to others as though I don't 'care' as much anymore, but that simply isn't it. It's my capacity to do these extra tasks which has diminished, and there's very little I can do about it. Do I still adore my pupils? Absolutely. Would I love to still be that teacher who goes to see their dance recitals and choir concerts at the weekends? Definitely. But we are human beings, and as I gaze with new-found sympathy at my tired colleagues as they stay in their classrooms during the Christmas disco, I have come to realise that being the 'fun, happy teacher' isn't a choice, it's a privilege.

Silent expectation #4: the increasing demands of parents

A recent post on my aforementioned social media group read as follows:

> Hello everyone. I've been a teacher for 10+ years and am getting sick of the workload and additional expectations. I'm just wondering if anyone has any thoughts on my current situation. At the start of the academic year, my headteacher gave the parents the email addresses of all teachers so we could be contacted directly by them. Over the last few weeks, I've experienced parents handing me and emailing me questionnaires and paperwork to complete for their child's private ADHD and ASD assessments, NHS OT assessments, dyslexia assessments etc. Like I haven't got enough work to do already. They have also started e-mailing for everyday questions that they could ask me in person or on parents' evening – yesterday I received 35 emails from parents alone.
>
> There's no way for management to monitor how much parents are asking of us unless we keep going to them to complain about it. When I did complain about one of the parent's requests (because it was one of the THREE questionnaires she requested for me to complete) the SENCo said she could sit with me to complete it. I explained I was perfectly competent enough to complete it, but felt there should be some limit on what parents could ask from us, without us being given additional time to do this extra work.
>
> Am I being unreasonable? It just feels like these parents are putting more and more on us like we have all the time in the world, and as management has given them a direct line to us, they can take themselves out of the equation.

When I was at school, my mother never liked to bother the teachers. What's more, if the teacher ever had anything to say to her, she listened. She never questioned my teachers or took my side over theirs because *they* were the teachers, and she respected that.

Times have changed. Where teachers used to be respected pillars of the community, we are now seen as 'providers of a service'. And much like other service providers, we receive many, many complaints. In my 11 years of teaching, have I made mistakes? Of course. But they were usually small errors resulting in very little inconvenience. I have never failed to keep a child in my care safe, and I have never, I feel, failed a child. The complaints I, and every other teacher I know, receive suggest that we are torturing these poor pupils. It is suddenly 'neglect' if we don't force their son to drink two bottles of water every day (when, madam, when?), and I simply don't care if I don't give someone else's daughter special treatment because her fourth cousin once-removed took her toy last week and she's now dysregulated. The demands and expectations of caregivers are growing, with fewer and fewer parents each year treating us with respect. It hurts, more to see it happening in real time, and no one seems to be brave enough to challenge it.

Now, are they still there?

You know, the SLT member who bulk ordered this book for your school to tick their 'well-being' box. They probably haven't got this far, so we'll be safe now. Firstly, I have to apologise for what I deem to be useful but were probably patronising lessons in happiness that you have no doubt heard before. The thing is, though, you have to do these things when writing a book for teachers. There's a formula. Take old, perfectly good advice and reframe it. Just like that last INSET day. How was that last INSET by the way? I think I saw you there. There was that motivational speaker who told us about the five signs of burn-out while we all checked them off in our heads. Then there was that inspirational author who told us incredible stories of his teaching career around the world. For a moment, we all remembered why we did it, with tears in our eyes and memories of 'that special pupil' whose life we changed. Then we all went home for the half-term break and received the customary 'INSET day survey' and 'holiday opening times' email despite just being told to switch off for the holidays.

Anyway, now I've got you, let's be real. Ofsted are, as has now been more publicly revealed, not dissimilar to the grand inquisitors of old. Dress it up however you like, but the term 'witch hunt' is a fair one. I have worked in and visited a large number of schools in my time to the point at which I can say with some confidence when a school is 'a good school'. So there I am, in the 'best' school I have ever taught in, and we get the call. I was at the tail end of a mild COVID infection at the time, and while the ball was in my court, it was suggested I come back the following day if I felt well enough. We were warned that our inspector was locally renowned for her delight in giving schools failing grades. First of all, why was this allowed? If a teacher had a reputation for failing more students than the rest, they'd be in a disciplinary hearing faster than you could say 'capability'. Yet this woman wore the role almost like a badge of honour. The first day was brutal. Strong, highly professional, dedicated people were left broken. Some nearly quit on the spot. Some cried. Adults, with years of experience, crying because of this one woman's judgement. In what other workplace would this be acceptable, and should it ever be acceptable anywhere, let alone expected, as it is? If you haven't been living under a rock for the past few years, I won't need to remind you about Ruth Perry – sadly not the first educational professional to take her own life due to the stress of Ofsted.

So now we come to the second half of our adventure, where I share with you some real-life examples and (hopefully) helpful exercises. Get your special pens and pencils ready!

Part II

Examples and exercises

Now we're alone, I thought I'd share with you some further examples from teachers I have met to reassure you that you are not alone in your quiet rage. More helpfully, it may give you some ideas for what to do if you are in a similar situation, as many of these circumstances have happened time and time again. I've also included some practical exercises, as every self-respecting self-help book includes exercises. Plus, it's always fun to write in a new book, isn't it? You can even use that free pen you got from your last CPD conference.

DOI: 10.4324/9781003506911-12

Exercise A Well-being in the workplace

Why has there been a sudden push for 'well-being in the workplace'? Is it because teachers have all collectively forgotten how to be cheerful? And why has public perception of teachers taken such a downward turn? Did they suddenly stop being good at their jobs? The reality is more nuanced, rendered almost invisible as a slower change over time. When I was at school (the 1990s – think PokÈmon cards, pogs, and pre-internet days – good lord, I miss the '90s) teachers were shown what I would call 'an appropriate' level of respect from society in general. If my teacher told my mother I'd done something against the rules (a very rare occurrence, might I add), my mum wouldn't argue with the teacher or complain to the school, as happens now, but she would apologise on behalf of her miscreant child. Now, if we need to give parents similar bad news, we need to phrase it in such a way as to not leave ourselves open to a lawsuit. Therefore, more often than not, the parents never truly realise the extent of what their child has done at the risk of litigation against the school. This gradual change over time has been created by several factors, including societal and cultural shifts over the generations. But this shift in attitude towards teaching has no doubt contributed to how 'worn down' teachers are now feeling. We're told to manage behaviour, but we aren't allowed to tell the parents the whole truth about this behaviour, waving the responsibility for that child's improvement solely at our door. We're told to phrase everything in a positive way to avoid complaints, and yet we are sent tens of emails every term from parents criticising our actions in a distinctly un-positive way. I have been threatened with violence by a father over something that happened before I even taught his son. A friend broke down in tears after being told by a mother, 'No wonder you couldn't have children.' A colleague was disciplined in a previous setting over something that never even occurred – the parents fabricated the entire story, but the parents were believed over the staff member. This is now 'normal' in our role, and we are expected to just accept it.

In parallel to this, as we know, the media seem to have turned on our profession somewhat in recent years. Concoct your own theories as to the motivations behind this, but my opinion is that publicly deriding us makes our arguments for higher wages and better working conditions less credible. Cynical? Perhaps. But is it therefore any wonder why 'well-being in the workplace' is now such a huge issue? It isn't the teachers who have changed but the job. Year after year, the goalposts are brought forward. Every parents' evening I get at least one person remarking, 'Didn't we learn this in Year 2 when we were seven? These children are four!' They are correct, of course. I also frequently hear, 'Why don't they start school later like they

DOI: 10.4324/9781003506911-13

do in Finland?' A separate debate, perhaps. But gone are the days of naptimes in Early Years and free play in Year 1. We don't have time for that now; there are too many things to learn! Something's got to give, we cry! And it has. It's the staff.

And so we arrive at 'well-being in the workplace'. At best, some posters on the backs of the toilet doors about a free 'well-being app' for staff. At worst, actively treating unhappy staff as the *problem* rather than the symptom of a broken system. While I have suggested in this book a great many ways to boost your own well-being in school, I am under no illusions. These steps will not change the problem at large. You, as an individual, cannot 'improve staff well-being' when you, as a staff, are being treated as you are.

So an exercise for you.

What would improve your well-being? Seriously think about it.

Firstly, note down everything you think of here:

_____
_____
_____
_____
_____
_____
_____
_____
_____
_____
_____
_____

Now separate those things into the following two categories:

1. 'Things I can achieve myself.' – This may be things such as 'take my lunch break' or 'spend more time playing with the children'.

    _____
    _____
    _____
    _____
    _____

2. 'Things SLT can assist me with.' – Now it's easy to be cynical here, but a good senior leader will *want* to improve the well-being of their staff. So team up with some colleagues here, and if you find yourselves with the same things in this section – take a punt and ask. They can only say no. Which brings us nicely to our next exercise.

    _____
    _____
    _____
    _____
    _____

Exercise B   Fight the power!

Full disclosure, I am left-leaning in terms of political allegiances, if that wasn't already abundantly clear. I grew up in a poor area and old, white, right-wing politicians generally scare me to death. Equally, however, I have an unhealthy fear of authority and confrontation, so striking also scares me to death. So I have been on both sides of this over the years. Essentially, it's up to you. But is it? Or do you have to factor in how many other teachers are striking so you're not alone in your dissent? Does your school remain neutral or even supportive towards striking members? Does your school have a union representative? Now feels like a good time to talk about my friend Ruth and her tenure as an NEU (National Education Union) representative at a large school in a deprived area.

When Ruth started at the school, she was fresh out of her first permanent position and keen to impress at a new school. It was a very large school that had semi-recently been academised by a notoriously 'business-first' academy trust. Within her first week, she received a phone call during a lesson. Initially, having a landline in each classroom felt like a fun novelty. The novelty wore off, but in this particular school, the phones were necessary for urgent behaviour concerns. Anyway, I digress. So there's Ruth, mid-input when her classroom phone rings. She pauses, slightly confused, and motions for her teaching assistant to take over for a second. A member of the office staff is on the other end of the phone and informs Ruth that the father of one of her pupils is on the line and wishes to make a complaint. So there she is, mid-lesson, with all the children listening, as she receives a complaint on the phone about something that happened before she even took up the post.

The following week, the school's union representative at the time held an informal union gathering at which she asked if anyone had any issues or concerns. Ruth brought up the event, and her colleagues were suitably shocked. The following day, Ruth received a terse word from the head. He informed her, rather defensively, that any future concerns would be more appropriately aired to him personally, and not 'behind his back' at a 'secretive gathering'. Now Ruth felt blindsided. She was, perhaps naively, under the impression that union meetings were accepted and healthy events at which to air these concerns. She realised quickly that this was not the 'culture' at this school.

Some years later, the aforementioned union rep (a real legend of her time, might I add) stepped down from her post, leaving no one keen to take on the controversial role. Ruth, being unable to say no, ended up taking it on. Just in time for the COVID pandemic to hit,

DOI: 10.4324/9781003506911-14

signalling one of the most difficult periods for union representatives in education history. Lucky Ruth! Her tenure began amongst a throng of 'good for you's and 'well done for stepping up's so it initially felt good. It felt like she was doing something to encourage positive change in her workplace. The higher-ups at the academy outwardly encouraged union reps to be involved in policy meetings and such, until, of course, they dissented. At this point, the tone became a little colder. However you feel about unions, though, the difference they made to Ruth's workplace was impressive. Due to the polite persistence of Ruth and her predecessors, the academy was forced to be more transparent with their pay scales, as well as make the pay scales more fair. This was one of many smaller (but equally appreciated) wins for the union during this time, which undoubtedly made life easier for the teachers and support staff at Ruth's school.

Now, I know what you're thinking – if I get one more text/email/carrier pigeon from 'Kevin and Mary at the NEU', I'm going to lose it. I am right there with you – during the pandemic, I felt like I heard from them more than my own family members, and then there were the Zoom meetings … goodness, the Zoom meetings. Painful memories. But their intentions, however occasionally misguided, remain in the best interests of school staff, and as such, Ruth thought she'd strike when the ballot was posted in 2023. The familiar feelings of guilt, of course, made her nauseous for several weeks. Would her class have to close? Would she be the only one? What would the parents say? What would her superiors say? Fortunately, her head was exceptionally supportive, and some of the parents even openly supported the teachers, which was nice. One of her 4-year-olds told her, 'My mum says you're basically having a day off', which was slightly disheartening but not inaccurate, I suppose.

Ultimately, you have to do what's best for you. That may involve not striking because you need to pay the mortgage, even though you believe in the cause. It might involve striking just because you're burnt out and need a day in bed. Whatever you choose, you have to make peace with your decision and stick to it. The reality is, however, that unless a large number of us fight against the conditions we find ourselves in, they won't change.

So here we have the second exercise.

Step 1: If you haven't already – join a union. Political opinions aside, if you are a teacher and you aren't in a union, any false allegation could end your career. It's just not worth the risk.

Step 2: Know your rights. Union or not, read up on The Burgundy Book. It's a handbook detailing all the national conditions of service for school teachers in England and Wales. It doesn't technically cover academy-run schools, however, they should still abide by it if they're decent employers. The Green Book is also an important document. It presents guidance issued by HM Treasury on how to appraise policies, programmes, and projects. It also guides the design and use of monitoring and evaluation before, during, and after implementation.

Step 3: You're stronger together – even if it's not in the form of union meetings, it's still important to regularly communicate with colleagues. If you're all having the same issues, you may be able to present a united front to management, giving you a stronger chance of success.

Example 1 So much for loyalty

Now I will introduce you to my friend Julia. Julia began teaching around the same time as me, and we got on well. She'd made her way through university as a single mother and remains one of the strongest people I know. She began working at a large academy-run school straight out of university, and I often heard tales of the similarities between her school and my own. Julia has now been at this school for nearly ten years and, throughout her time there, has been promised two promotions she wasn't given. The first time this happened, she was turned down because she didn't have any Key Stage 2 (ages 7-11) experience. To soften the blow, she was summarily thrust from the younger year groups (at the time, Year 2) straight into Year 6 (ages 10-11) with the promise of 'next time it's yours'. Anyway, the next time it was given to a newer male teacher who had only started there the year before but had 'experience in other schools', which Julia did not. So much for loyalty.

The sad thing is that teachers like Julia don't always get rewarded for loyalty. Their loyalty is their weakness because academies know they won't go anywhere no matter how poorly they treat them. Thankfully, things don't always work out this way, and some schools reward loyalty. But if your employer is the sort to favour fresh blood over staff with a history, it may be prudent to at least hint to your superiors that you are keeping your options open. This isn't to say, of course, that every rejected promotion opportunity should be seen as a systemic issue, but you do get the feel for a place after a while. We've all heard of those academies who like to 'turf out' the older 'expensive' teachers in favour of new hires who can be 'moulded to the academy's vision'. If you're a new teacher, then you can use this to your advantage, just be aware that your value may diminish as your price tag increases. It shouldn't be about money, but with government cuts and tightened budgets, these things unfortunately come into play.

Eventually, Julia moved on to take a senior position at another school which, thankfully, appreciated her talents. She found herself happier, not because of the senior position, but because she was in a setting that valued experience. While there's no denying it's tough all over, a different setting may offer the change of perspective you need to find that elusive spark of joy again.

A similar thing happened to me some years ago. A common phrase in self-help circles back when I was at university was 'compare and despair'. This is not inaccurate and can certainly apply in teaching. In my previous position, I had been teaching in Key Stage 1 for around five years when I applied for the head of year post. I didn't get it, and no reason was given. It was

DOI: 10.4324/9781003506911-15

given to a newer employee with less experience. This happened three times over my six years at the school. I couldn't help but assume something was wrong with me. I was told they would happily give me the post tomorrow, they just ... didn't. Every time. It can be hard not to take that personally. However, there are several factors which could have led to this situation. I could have had the wrong *kind* of experience – I have always specialised in the younger years, and they could have been looking for someone used to older children. It is important not to judge those who get the position instead of you, as often they are all extremely skilled teachers and deserving of their roles. Comparing yourself with others is easy but dangerous. It turned out that the reasons for my rejection were exactly that – the first position was in Year 5, which was far higher up than I had ever taught. The second, I now know, had already been given before interviews, which were a formality. This happens upsettingly often in schools. The final time, it was given to my friend, who is to this day one of the most brilliant young teachers I've had the honour of working with. She's one of those people who makes it look easy, but you can't help but like her because she's also incredibly kind. So I didn't begrudge that one at all. I would have done the same.

So where it is easy to see a pattern of rejection, take a moment to remember that not everything in life – or in school – is about you.

Example 2   School values

Another colleague, Sam, began his teaching career in a particularly religious Church of England school. He attended a church school as a child, and while he wasn't religious himself, he respected the school's stance and taught his pupils Christian values as directed (although he always felt uncomfortable telling children that they didn't have a choice but to believe in God and Jesus). Everything was fine for the first few months, and Sam was even invited to a colleague's house for a work social. While there, one of the older members of staff started making homophobic comments, and Sam's heart fell. One of the other teachers at the gathering knew Sam was gay, but he hadn't told everyone at the school yet. His colleague looked apologetically at Sam and mouthed 'sorry'. Sam smiled weakly but was quiet for the rest of the night.

A few months later, a new chair of governors was appointed. A deeply religious man, his first action was to create a 'Christian audit' for the staff. This would involve phoning the vicars of each of the staff members, enquiring about their level of commitment to the church, as well as a couple of lifestyle questions. It was at this point that Sam knew he was in trouble. At the very start of his career, he didn't have the confidence or experience to realise that the school couldn't legally force him out for being gay. So some months and several awkward conversations later, Sam hastily handed in his resignation and jumped into the next available job he could, supply teaching. He was still living with his mother, so the unstable income wasn't a disaster, but the blip in his job history would impede his job prospects for years to come, as he struggled to find another permanent teaching position. He hadn't been forced out per se, but he had certainly been made to feel as though he didn't have a choice other than to jump or be pushed.

If you find yourself in this situation, there is an obvious solution. One that, sadly, Sam didn't know he could take. You can absolutely take them to court on this. It's illegal, unacceptable, and frankly, quite un-Christian, as many Christians would agree I'm sure. Now this is not a tirade against religious schools. They all vary wildly in terms of doctrine and practice. Why, my ex-partner taught at a school with a regularly attending vicar who frequently asked her how I (her girlfriend) was doing. So please don't mistake my example to be an attack. But it is also important that, when you go into a school, you try to get a feel for what you might be letting yourself in for. When the job advertisements say 'visits welcome', they really mean it. The best thing I did was supply at the beginning of my career – because you never really get a feel for the school on a visit alone – you see what the head wants you to see. But supplying

DOI: 10.4324/9781003506911-16

at a school, you very quickly get to see the things others do not, which can be positive or negative.

Further information on religious schools in the UK, for those of you unaware of the slightly confusing system we have going on over here:

> In the United Kingdom, the landscape of education is diverse, encompassing both religious and state-funded schools, each with its own distinct characteristics, advantages, and challenges. Understanding the differences between these two types of institutions is crucial for navigating the educational landscape and making informed decisions about where to teach or enrol children. Religious schools, often referred to as faith schools, are institutions that are affiliated with a particular religious denomination or faith tradition. These schools may receive funding from religious organisations, as well as from the government, and typically incorporate religious teachings and practices into their curriculum and ethos. In the UK, religious schools are prevalent across various faith traditions, including Christianity, Islam, Judaism, and Sikhism, among others.

One of the key features of religious schools is their emphasis on imparting religious values, beliefs, and teachings alongside academic instruction. For many parents and students, this can be a significant draw, providing a sense of cultural continuity and spiritual guidance within the educational environment. Additionally, religious schools may offer a sense of community and belonging for families who share the same faith tradition, fostering strong bonds among students, parents, and educators. However, religious schools also raise important questions about inclusivity, diversity, and the separation of church and state. Critics argue that these institutions may promote sectarianism and reinforce social divisions by prioritising students of a particular religious background. Furthermore, concerns have been raised about the potential for discrimination in admissions and employment practices, particularly regarding the treatment of students and staff who do not adhere to the school's religious ethos. For example, I attended a C of E school as a child (Church of England, Christian), and one of my earliest memories remains being told off, repeatedly, for being unable to draw a picture of my godparents because I didn't have any.

'Every child at this school has godparents, when were you Christened?' I had no answers. On the walk home, my mother reaffirmed that no, I was never christened, so I had been told off all afternoon for, essentially, an assumption. I was six.

In contrast, state-funded schools, also known as public schools, are institutions that receive funding directly from the government and are not affiliated with any religious denomination or faith tradition. These schools are required to adhere to national educational standards and regulations, offering a secular curriculum that is accessible to students from diverse backgrounds and beliefs. State schools play a vital role in promoting inclusivity, equality, and social cohesion within society by providing education that is free from religious indoctrination. They welcome students of all faiths and none, fostering an environment of tolerance, respect, and understanding.

However, state schools also face their own set of challenges, including issues related to funding, resources, and educational attainment. Budget constraints and overcrowding can impact the quality of education offered, while disparities in funding between schools in affluent and disadvantaged areas can exacerbate inequalities in academic achievement and social mobility. This is why many non-religious parents still push to have their children attend religious schools, which are often seen as 'better'.

Overall, both religious and state schools contribute to the rich tapestry of education in the UK, offering families a range of options to suit their values, beliefs, and priorities. While religious schools provide a sense of cultural identity and spiritual guidance for some, state schools offer a foundation of secular education that promotes inclusivity and diversity for all.

Example 3   The school bully

Sarah was a quiet girl. She loved teaching and she had been doing it long enough now to feel confident in her day-to-day work. One September, her old head of year retired and was replaced by a male teacher from in a different year group. This man, Victor, was someone Sarah had seen around school but never worked with. Granted, alarm bells should have rung early on when colleagues warned her to 'watch your back around him'. Sarah, though, always saw the best in people and decided to ignore said warnings.

This was a mistake

According to the Education Support organisation, a survey carried out by the trade union NASUWT in 2019 found that four out of every five teachers said they had experienced bully-ing at work. Sarah couldn't believe it at first. How was she being bullied … as an adult? But the subtle gaslighting and master manipulation made that year a living hell for the previously confident teacher until she reached a point where she ended up questioning her ability to continue in her career. Friends told her that Victor was just threatened by Sarah's abilities, but this brought no comfort. She just wanted it to stop. Unfortunately, due to her quietness and nervousness, she knew she wouldn't be able to out-talk Victor if it came to it, so she kept her head down and tried to carry on.

But it was never enough. As quiet and invisible as she tried to be, there wouldn't be a day that passed without a snide comment in the staffroom ('I thought you knew how to teach art. I'm so sorry I didn't explain the lesson more slowly') or public humiliation in front of her class ('Children, remind Miss Atkins of why we always use a ruler to underline our headings'). After a decade of teaching, Sarah quit the profession halfway through that year.

If you ever find yourself in this situation, which, if the data is to be believed, you almost definitely have, I implore you to call Education Support. They are a wonderful organisation with the manifesto: 'Our mission is to improve the mental health and wellbe-ing of teachers and education staff. We believe that better mental health leads to better education.' They have specific pages on bullying in the workplace and are a non-biased port of call for any school-related concerns. While Victor may well have been threatened by Sarah, as she had more years of experience in the year group which he was newly entering at its helm, there is never an excuse to treat colleagues in this way. Schools are difficult and hostile enough places to work without this – your colleagues should be one

DOI: 10.4324/9781003506911-17

of the best things about your day, and certainly not the thing you come to work feeling nauseous about.

I myself have experienced being treated poorly by colleagues. Once, and now I know this particular woman to have been going through a divorce, so I do sympathise, but I was shouted at in front of my entire class of 5- and 6-year-olds not clearing out the previous teacher's possessions from my cupboard. She just needed to take her pain out on someone, and that someone happened to be me. Eventually, I learned of her situation and forgave her, but do remember to check yourself – am I the bully? Sometimes we forget that our 'teacher voice' isn't for our colleagues and can blur those boundaries. I have had line managers who have taken umbrage with my age, my gender, and my sexuality before, but those were their issues, not mine, and as a helpful therapist pointed out at the time – you don't need to catch the ball they are throwing at you.

Let me explain. This was during a time at which I was being regularly criticised and shouted at – publicly, I might add – by a line manager going through a difficult time. My therapist at the time told me to think of her words like a basketball (or netball, football, whichever your sport). So whenever she came in to tell me, oh, I don't know, that my display wasn't straight enough, I could choose not to 'catch that ball'. I couldn't outright ignore a superior, but she meant that I didn't have to take that criticism on board. Obviously make sure that the criticism isn't founded in a truth you need to address first (but thankfully, my display was spirit-level straight), but once you know the criticism to be unfounded – drop the ball. You don't need to carry that around. They needed to throw it at someone, that's their issue, not yours.

So I suppose the lesson from this example is – that sometimes it's okay to drop a few balls.

Another way to deal with this situation is, of course, to use it as a lesson – let it make you even stronger. And that's precisely what my friend Emily did.

Once upon a time, in a quaint little town nestled amidst rolling hills and whispering forests, there was a school where the air hummed with the promise of knowledge and the laughter of children. Among the dedicated educators who walked its halls was Ms Emily Hartley, a gentle soul with a passion for nurturing young minds. Ms Hartley's classroom was a sanctuary of creativity and learning, where every child felt valued and heard. Her days were filled with the joy of teaching, until one fateful September when a new parent, Mrs Victoria Hawthorne, entered her world like a storm cloud on the horizon.

Victoria Hawthorne was a force to be reckoned with – a woman accustomed to getting her way, with a sharp tongue and a steely gaze that could pierce through even the thickest facade of confidence. From the moment she stepped into the school, whispers of caution fluttered in the air, but Emily, ever the optimist, chose to give her the benefit of the doubt. Yet it didn't take long for Mrs Hawthorne's true colours to emerge. Behind closed doors, she waged a campaign of subtle intimidation and manipulation against Ms Hartley, casting doubt upon her teaching methods and undermining her authority at every turn.

At first, Emily tried to brush off the snide remarks and passive-aggressive jabs, but as the days turned into weeks and the weeks into months, the weight of Mrs Hawthorne's hostility bore down upon her like an oppressive shadow. The once vibrant spirit of Ms Hartley began to dim, replaced by a gnawing sense of self-doubt and anxiety. No matter how hard she tried to maintain her composure, there was always another barb waiting to strike, whether it was a condescending comment during parents' evenings or a thinly veiled threat veiled behind a saccharine smile.

Despite the support of her colleagues and the reassurances of friends, Emily found herself trapped in a suffocating web of fear and uncertainty. She began to question her worth as a teacher, wondering if perhaps she wasn't cut out for the challenges of the classroom after all. But deep within her heart, a flicker of resilience still burned. Summoning the courage she thought she had lost, Emily reached out to her support network for guidance. With their encouragement, she found the strength to confront Mrs Hawthorne, all the while maintaining a calm and professional demeanour.

In the end, it was not Emily who crumbled beneath the weight of Mrs Hawthorne's cruelty, but the bully herself, confronted by the unwavering resolve of not just Ms Hartley, but her deputy head and even fellow parents who had seen what had been going on and were disgusted with the behaviour. With her head held high, Emily reclaimed her voice and her dignity, emerging from the ordeal stronger and more resilient than ever before.

And though the scars of that time would linger, they served as a reminder of the power of perseverance and the incredible power of supportive colleagues. Would she have been able to face her bully alone? Unlikely. But in that moment, surrounded by colleagues and parents who believed in her, she finally started to believe again that she was a good teacher.

Exercise C   Rate your workplace

We've all been given the surveys,

> Ofsted has asked us to do a staff survey but this is *not* the time to air your dirty laundry.
> Positive responses only please.

Cue the negative responses and subsequent disciplinary meetings with colleagues, despite the promise that the surveys were anonymous. Anyway, this time you can be honest with yourself. Perhaps you're really happy with your school, and this should tell you. I'm not saying you have to be negative here – just be honest. No one is looking … probably.

For each of the following statements, write a number corresponding to how you feel about the statement:

Not at all – 1
Not really – 2
Sometimes – 3
Mostly – 4
Definitely – 5

Statements to rate:

My school cares about its staff –
My school listens to its staff –
My school is run fairly –
I would recommend my school to other staff –
I am happy at my school –

Now add up your score and compare it to the below statements:

5–10 – Oh dear. Look for another job. Surely nothing is worth this?
10–15 – I don't know what to tell you, there are better schools out there, honestly.
15–20 – Okay, things could be worse
20–25 – Brilliant news, you are in one of the good ones. Stick with it, and tell your friends.

DOI: 10.4324/9781003506911-18

The reality is that even in the best schools, conditions are tough. Ultimately, the profession is under attack by those much higher up than the headteachers or even the academy CEOs. So if you are in a school that you feel truly supports you, know that you are in a better position than most. Hold on for dear life.

Conversely, if your school has scored poorly, think about why that is. Has your school fallen on hard times? Are you having trouble filling places and therefore in the midst of a financial crisis? Has there been a change in management? Have you just joined a new academy? It may not be anyone's fault that you are where you are, but you still need to put yourself first. It may seem obvious, but you cannot be a happy teacher if you aren't happy at your school.

If you are unsure as to where you fall on this dizzying spectrum of teacher happiness, let me give you two examples – you can think about which resonates with you more strongly.

Claire's story

Claire sighed as she reluctantly picked up the staff survey, her heart heavy with disillusionment and disappointment. For the past few years, she had been teaching at Oakridge Academy, a once-promising institution that had fallen on hard times. As she glanced down at the list of statements, a wave of bitterness washed over her, punctuated by a sense of resignation and despair.

'My school cares about its staff,' she read aloud, her voice tinged with bitterness. With a weary hand, Claire circled 'Not really', the words catching in her throat as she recalled the countless instances of neglect and indifference that had eroded her faith in the institution. From budget cuts that decimated support services to a culture of blame and finger-pointing among senior leadership, Oakridge Academy seemed to prioritise profits over people, leaving teachers like Claire feeling undervalued and unsupported.

'My school listens to its staff,' she muttered bitterly, marking 'Not at all' with a sense of resignation. At Oakridge, the voices of teachers were routinely silenced and dismissed, drowned out by the deafening roar of bureaucracy and corporate interests. Despite her best efforts to advocate for change and improvement, Claire had grown accustomed to the futility of speaking out, knowing that her concerns would fall on deaf ears. As she reached the final question, Claire hesitated, her heart heavy with uncertainty. 'I am happy at my school,' she murmured, her hand hovering uncertainly over the checkboxes. In the end, she left it blank, unable to muster the courage to commit to either affirmation or denial. For Claire, happiness at Oakridge Academy was a distant dream, a mirage shimmering on the horizon of an increasingly bleak landscape.

As she submitted her survey, Claire felt a sense of resignation wash over her, knowing that the road ahead would be fraught with challenges and obstacles. Despite her longing for change and improvement, she couldn't shake the sinking feeling that Oakridge Academy was a sinking ship, dragging her down with it into the depths of despair and disillusionment.

Fiona's story

As Fiona sat down to complete the staff survey, a sense of gratitude washed over her. She had been teaching at St Mary's Primary School for over a decade, and every year, her appreciation for the institution seemed to deepen. With each tick of the box, she reflected on the myriad ways in which her school had supported her, nurtured her growth, and fostered a sense of belonging.

'My school cares about its staff,' she mused, confidently circling 'Definitely'. From the compassionate leadership of the headteacher to the camaraderie among colleagues, St Mary's exuded a palpable sense of care and compassion that permeated every aspect of school life. Whether it was through regular check-ins with the staff well-being team or thoughtful gestures of appreciation during Teacher Appreciation Week, Fiona knew that she was valued and supported.

'My school listens to its staff,' she continued, marking 'Definitely' without hesitation. At St Mary's, the voices of teachers were not only heard but actively sought out and respected. From staff meetings to curriculum planning sessions, Fiona always felt empowered to share her ideas and concerns, knowing that they would be met with thoughtful consideration and open dialogue. As she reached the final question, Fiona couldn't help but smile. 'I am happy at my school,' she affirmed, ticking 'Definitely' with unwavering certainty. For Fiona, St Mary's was more than just a workplace – it was a second home, a sanctuary of learning and laughter where she felt inspired, supported, and cherished.

As she submitted her survey, Fiona felt a sense of pride swell within her. Despite the challenges and uncertainties that often plagued the teaching profession, she knew that she was exactly where she was meant to be – at a school that truly cared for its staff and fostered a culture of excellence and empowerment.

Nya's story

Nya sat down with the staff survey, feeling neither overwhelmed with joy nor burdened with despair. She had been teaching at Greenfield Community School for several years now, and while it wasn't perfect, it also wasn't a disaster. As she glanced over the statements, she found herself navigating a middle ground, neither wholly satisfied nor wholly dissatisfied with her school.

'My school cares about its staff,' she pondered, her pen hovering over the checkboxes. After a moment's consideration, Nya settled on 'Mostly'. While Greenfield Community School did make efforts to support its staff through staff development programs and occasional wellness initiatives, there were times when she felt that more could be done to address individual concerns and challenges.

'My school listens to its staff,' she continued, marking 'Sometimes' with a thoughtful expression. At Greenfield, the lines of communication were open, but there were moments when Nya felt as though her voice got lost in the shuffle. While she appreciated the opportunity to share her ideas and feedback, she couldn't shake the feeling that some issues fell on deaf ears or were met with token gestures rather than meaningful action. As she reached the final question, Nya paused, her gaze drifting to the blank space beside 'I am happy at my school'. It was a question she grappled with daily, torn between moments of contentment and moments of frustration. In the end, she circled 'Sometimes', acknowledging the ebb and flow of emotions that coloured experience at Greenfield Community School.

As she submitted her survey, Nya felt a sense of acceptance settle over her. While Greenfield may not have been the perfect school, it was her school – a place where she could make a difference, grow as an educator, and forge connections with her colleagues and students. Despite its imperfections, Greenfield Community School was a place of opportunity and possibility, and for Nya, that was enough.

For me, Nya's story is certainly relatable. Claire's story would have been true for me at a time, but thankfully no longer, and Fiona's ... well, I heard you all laugh as you read it, but I have supplied in one school (yes, 1 out of around 50) where they really seemed to have cracked the code and the staff were genuinely happy (see Chapter 9). This isn't about aligning yourself with one particular scenario, necessary, but using them to reflect on your own situation and position. Where are you? What are you feeling? What can *you* do to change that? If the answer is 'find a better school', then I urge you to try. They are desperate for teachers out there.

Exercise D   Problem-solving

All credit for this exercise must go to a fellow teacher and head of computing. She got the idea from a Google conference up in London (one of the perks of subject leadership).

For this exercise you will need:

- Sticky notes
- Pencils
- A list of your current 'problems'

Method:

Step 1: Think of the scenarios in your life in which you encounter problems. For example:
  - o Arriving at school
  - o During a lesson
  - o During planning time
  - o Break time
  - o Lunchtime
  - o After school
  - o Marking work
  - o A staff meeting
  - o Sunday night
  - o 3 am and you just can't sleep

Step 2: Within each of these scenarios, think of the specific problems you face. Assign each problem to a sticky note. These problems might be things you encounter in your everyday working life, such as 'I can never find parking' or 'I need to phone a difficult parent'. You don't need to worry about the specificity of these just yet. Just write as many as you can think of.

Step 3: Now, arrange these problem sticky notes from 'smallest to biggest', so to speak, from left (least concern) to right (most concern).

Step 4: Next, while keeping your sticky notes in a horizontal line, rank them by how many people they impact. For example, not finding a parking space may only affect you, so move it vertically down. Losing your teaching assistant to budget cuts, however, affects both you and the 30 children in your class, so move that one up. You should

DOI: 10.4324/9781003506911-19

now have a list of problems arranged in a visual order from least to most concerning, allowing you to prioritise.

Step 5: Look at your problems, look at where they lie, and circle the one you want to tackle
first. It may help to do this activity with colleagues, as workshopping problems
together can provide the most creative solutions.

Step 6: Once you have solved the first problem (or at least tried your best), move on to the
next one, taking into account urgency and the number of people affected.

While this activity may seem overwhelming at first – nobody likes seeing all of their problems
laid out in front of them – it can lighten the mental load and allow you to compartmentalise
a little bit. Instead of a ball of string worrying around in our brain, you now have some inter-
pretable lines. Some of these problems may not be solvable, and that's okay. You may never
find that water bottle, or indeed parking. What can you do to support yourself with those
things? An electric scooter to scoot from your parking space, miles away from school, like
a boss each morning while your pupils shout out 'sick ride, Miss G' as you glide past in your
Disney cardigan and canvas tote. A new water bottle covered in glitter and unicorns because
making 4-year-olds jealous is a perk of the job? Not everything is fixable, but everything can
be addressed.

Example 4   The teacher's pet

It was a cold, grey day in a small British seaside town. Gwen was getting ready for school, as usual. Her brother, Matthew, was eating Cheerios. Gwen was fretting about which socks to wear. She could wear her new ones, which were the whitest pair of clothing she had ever owned, or her regular, greying ones with the long thread. Gwen found change difficult and so opted for the latter, again. The walk to school was all uphill, and Gwen enjoyed looking at the big billboards at around the halfway mark. Last week they had been advertising the new strip club in town, but now they were promoting the local radio station. Gwen enjoyed catching them in between advertisements when you could see the layers of billboards past.

When she got to school, Gwen made the familiar trudge through the cloakroom. She found her label (on the floor again), hung up her coat, and wandered into class, trying not to attract attention. She settled down in her favourite spot - the book corner - and located her current favourite book. It was an antique copy of *The Water Babies* by Charles Kingsley. One of her very favourite things was to listen to her mother read it to her at bedtime, and looking at the pictures helped her feel the safe familiarity of home.

As the last of the pupils sat down, Mrs Piddington began the register. She was second and always resented the boy who came before her.

'Reuben Berry?'

'Good morning, Mrs Piddington.'

'Gwen Boyd?'

'Good morning, Mrs Piddington, I love your earrings.'

The class' eyes collectively rolled. As an adult, Gwen would come to cringe as she remembered that moment, but she had always been the teacher's pet. There was just something about teachers that she admired. Not all of them, of course. Gwen had studied under what she would later describe as 'a very mixed bag' of educational practitioners, but Mrs Piddington was a favourite. She was a supply teacher but frequently covered Gwen's class, and while the other children thought she was boring and stuffy, Gwen felt as s though Mrs Piddington was one of the people who most cared about her in the world. She always listened, and she was the first to congratulate her when she got into grammar school. More than that though, she was the first person to believe in her.

DOI: 10.4324/9781003506911-20

'Of course, I knew you'd get in.' Gwen was so surprised to hear those words because never before had anyone had quite so much faith in her to do … anything. So Gwen respected her teachers and, yes, was what her peers used to call a 'boffin' and a 'suck up', but Gwen didn't mind. She could always escape into her books, and while she would have liked friends, she learned pretty quickly that being smart and having friends were mutually exclusive in her particular school. And she decided that she would rather be smart than be friends with girls who cared more about dolphins than books.

The years rolled along, and Gwen would pass through other classes and other teachers. Many of which, through no real fault of theirs, sort of forgot she was there most of the time. She didn't really speak, got on with her work quietly, and didn't cause a fuss – a teacher's dream. On those rare occasions when Gwen was noticed, however, it lit up her world.

Secondary school was, shall we say, variable. A grammar school for girls with morals firmly stuck in the 1950s – her mother and aunt had both attended the institution, while her father had gone to the neighbouring boys' school. Gwen enjoyed the learning, for the most part, but struggled with some of the teachers. One, a religious education teacher, was known for shouting and scolding his classes en masse. Another was seen throwing a chair. It was a frightening prospect for a shy 11-year-old, and while Gwen didn't get into any real trouble while she was there, it wasn't exactly a nurturing place to grow up. Thankfully, a handful of teachers seemed to genuinely like teenagers and made her time there more pleasant. The choir was a safe space for her, and she even, finally, made a small group of friends – fellow 'misfits' who didn't fit in with the rest. As she grew, she realised more and more that not all teachers were created equal, and which ones were worthy of her respect.

Towards the end of her time at grammar school, shortly before escaping to a separate sixth-form college, things deteriorated. Having followed the rules and been liked, for the most part, by her teachers for her entire school career, things suddenly changed. She had realised, one lunchtime, that she was a lesbian. Quite the realisation, you may think, but Gwen was a little slow off the mark and should have realised this years ago. However, it was when she began dating a fellow student at the school that things got a bit tricky. The consensus amongst staff was that lesbianism was 'unbecoming of a girl at our institution' and that, frankly, Gwen needed to 'get over it'. Gwen did not. Well, after one teacher threatened to tell Gwen's parents (to whom she was not yet out) and another, shockingly, fabricated a false rumour about Gwen and her then-girlfriend which spread around the school (they had been playing the piano together in a practice room – the teacher implied it had been an awful lot more), Gwen had decided that teachers, for the most part, could no longer be trusted. If it wasn't for Mr Winrow sitting them both down and showing some humanity (essentially, he told them to be who they were but not to make it obvious because other teachers didn't like it), she might have given up altogether.

So Gwen moved on to sixth form, then university, where her experience with teachers, sadly, only got worse. Her music technology teacher announced, on their first day, that he didn't want to teach but needed the money.

Great. The highest mark in that class for the final exam was a D. He taught none of the course material. Luckily Gwen managed to make that up to a B with her coursework.

Her singing teacher at university refused to teach her because she was an alto and not a soprano – which just means her vocal range was low to medium and not very high. This is perfectly fine to anyone else you ask – Adele is an alto, for goodness sake. But this man – the man who would be giving her a final grade for her music degree – sent her to an ear, nose, and throat specialist, to have a camera put down her throat, to see if there was 'anything wrong' with her voice. There wasn't. She was just an alto. At this revelation, he refused to teach her. In retrospect, this was incredibly unprofessional, and he should have been spoken to, but Gwen just wanted her degree. So with no teacher (and consequently no accompanist), she accompanied herself for her final exam and sang a song she wrote herself. The teacher who had told her she couldn't pass the performance exam with 'that voice' was sick that day and therefore not on the judging panel. She got a 2:i. On her own.

One of her English professors was similarly unenthusiastic in her praises for Gwen's passions. Gwen loved to write, but this teacher informed her that she needed to go to a writing tutor as her writer's voice would never pass her course. The writing tutor was baffled by this and said she saw no problem with Gwen's work. When her final exam was anonymously graded, Gwen received a first from the same professor who had belittled her.

You might wonder, at this point, what Gwen went on to do. Would it shock you to know she became a teacher? It was never a dream or a plan, but Gwen wanted to be a music therapist, and there were, at the time, no jobs in that field due to budget cuts and shifting government attitudes to 'creative therapies'. So she sort of fell into teaching. She loved the children and desperately wanted to be the next 'Miss Honey' from Matilda. The thing is, though, if Miss Honey was teaching nowadays, she'd be on capability for not managing behaviour effectively or covering the curriculum in enough detail. But still, that was what Gwen wanted to do.

So Gwen was the teacher's pet who became the teacher. She began her career at a small village school, moving to a busy, business-like academy before ending up in a large, community primary school. She lived through many of the examples within this book but ended up in a good place. She was so happy that she even began writing a book, *How to Be a Happy Teacher*. Well, it was less than a year into this post that things changed for Gwen, and she went from feeling on top of the world to being buried beneath it. Gwen abandoned her book – how could she write about being a happy teacher when she no longer was one?

Gwen sunk into a depression that affected not only her work but her personal life as well. She abandoned her hobbies, friends drifted away as she became 'too sad' to be around, and Gwen found herself coming home each night only to go to bed, exhausted from the mental struggle she faced each day. Was it just one thing that had beaten her or a combination of events? Her whole life, she'd gone from worshipping her teachers, to being let down by them, to becoming one, to feeling like a failed one. Her friends begged her not to give up on her decade-long career because of one person, but Gwen wasn't strong enough to fight it. Years of trying to be Miss Honey only to see Trunchbull after Trunchbull rise to the top had broken her.

Gwen lay in the darkness, staring at the pages before her. What would she do now? How could she be happy again? She read back her own advice.

She phoned Education Support, who reassured and advised her.

She spoke to her colleagues who had been through entirely similar situations.

She threw herself into playtimes with abandon, shoved her paperwork to the side, and spent time with the children who, without her prompting, reassured her that she was 'the best teacher ever'. (Children are emphatic like that; it's a real mood booster until you realise they say that to all their teachers.)

She spoke to her friends about what might make her happy, *truly* happy.

And she compromised. She didn't leave. But she compromised. Gwen decided to transition to part-time teaching to focus on a career in writing, with a spot of singing on the side. That was what Gwen needed, at that moment, to be a happy teacher. She wrote 'Part Two' of her book, with real-world examples and exercises, to support other teachers like herself, and she threw herself into her writing.

Oh, Gwen is me. Obviously. I didn't want to be a hypocrite and pretend that I was the all-knowing wizard of teacher happiness – extolling lessons to you silly, stressed-out teachers from on high. No, I wanted to show you that I am just like you. Tired, burnt-out, underappreciated, and lost. Is that what you were expecting? Neither was I. But sadly, there is no magic cure or miracle tome to our plight. We must all find our way to happiness, and all I can hope is that I have helped you on your way to find yours.

We change lives every day in what we do. We might not be noticed or praised for it – instead, we may be constantly criticised – but I can assure you, you will have left this world a better place because you chose a career that improved the lives of hundreds of children (thousands if you teach for long enough!)

Good luck out there, you're a damn superhero.

Printed in the United States
by Baker & Taylor Publisher Services

Printed in the United States
by Baker & Taylor Publisher Services